IF HEAVEN IS SO WONDERFUL . . .
WHY COME HERE?

IF HEAVEN IS
SO WONDERFUL . . .

WHY COME HERE?

How to Discover
Our "Whole Being"

JOHN L. BROOKER

BLUE DOLPHIN

Published by Blue Dolphin Publishing, Inc.
P.O. Box 8, Nevada City, CA 95959
Orders: 1-800-643-0765
Web: www.bluedolphinpublishing.com

ISBN: 1-57733-143-5

Library of Congress Cataloging-in-Publication Data

Brooker, John L., 1923–
    If heaven is so wonderful— why come here? : how to
discover our "whole being" / John L. Brooker.
        p. cm.
Includes bibliographical references.
    ISBN 1-57733-143-5 (pbk. : alk. paper)
    1. Spiritualism. I. Title.

    BF1261.2.B76 2003
    133.9—dc22
                                                    2003023462

Printed in the United States of America

10   9   8   7   6   5   4   3   2

TABLE OF CONTENTS

ACKNOWLEDGMENTS

I WISH TO ACKNOWLEDGE the contributions to the work of the many guides and teachers from the spirit world. Their wisdom, patience, and encouragement has been invaluable.

I also thank all the trance mediums who have brought the wisdom from the world of spirit over the years and made this work possible. Without the contributions of these sensitive people we would be deprived of a source of knowledge of the life to come.

I wish to thank my wife Naomi for her support and patience. Naomi was responsible for proofreading my work and adding some excellent ideas as the book developed.

Also, I thank Dr. Dean Schrock, a friend and fellow traveler, for his suggestions when he proofread the manuscript.

INTRODUCTION

MANY BOOKS HAVE BEEN WRITTEN about life after death, most of them from a religious point of view. This book is the result of many years of research and discussion with discarnate entities about life in the spirit world from their point of view.

Some people believe they have to travel to a foreign country or find some exotic teacher to find the inner self. I want to emphasize that it is not necessary. One can learn all about the inner self and have mystical experiences without leaving the chair on which he is sitting to read this book.

If a person is told that a certain spot has spiritual powers, he may go there expecting to have an enlightening experience. An expectation or a spiritual frame of mind may produce the desired effect. Meditation can produce the same effect and save him the trouble of the trip.

I have found that spiritual truth is within us and costs nothing.

For over fifty years I have communicated with people from the next world. Guides and teachers from spirit have taught me what life is like in the spirit world, and through their teaching I have gathered the knowledge contained in this book.

I have included some basic assumptions to form a framework for the book. A person wishing to develop spiritually can use these as a set of questions to be researched.

1. There is no death.
2. We create our own reality by the thoughts we think.
3. We are always linked to the divine essence called God.
4. We are infinite beings manifesting temporarily in this dimension.
5. We create time to enable us to experience the life we have chosen for this incarnation.
6. We are here on earth to bring the great power of love as it is in heaven.
7. There is nothing but love and acceptance in the spirit world.
8. Good and evil are value judgments based on what is acceptable or unacceptable to the observer.
9. There is no judgment or punishment in the spirit world except that which is self-created.
10. We have to live with who we are, and self-punishment will bring growth through experience.

Much of the information in this work was obtained using different trance mediums in the meditation groups that I have conducted over the past fifty years.

For trance to be successful, the medium has to be mentally quiet. The medium's mind has to be poised in a mental no-man's-land. Once this is established, concepts can be sent from the person in the spirit world, through the aura of the medium. No one from spirit can enter into the body of another being. All communication is by telepathy.

There is no such thing as possession in this work.

There have been many teachers who have spoken to me over the years, and the information in this book is the result of their teachings.

I have asked many spirit guides to describe what happens when a person makes the transition to spirit at death. There is much unlearning to be done before we complete the process.

I have tried to avoid talking about particular religions because it is too selective and limiting. There are no such divisions once one is free of the earth/astral plane influences.

Religion creates a code of social conduct, and we would have very few guidelines for self-improvement without it. However, it is limited to the earth and astral planes.

I wish people to understand that we are a small part of our "whole being" that comes to have a life on this planet. Other parts of our whole being also exist on other levels or dimensions at the same time.

The whole purpose of this book is to give an accurate report of the teachings I have gathered over the years. Mostly the book is my interpretation of the spiritual teachings I have received from many different teachers, from both earth and spirit.

I have learned that advanced souls in spirit are not concerned with names and titles. They can assume any identity because of their understanding of the oneness of all things. We will be able to do the same thing when we have advanced to the spirit world and have the same understanding.

This book is not only about the spirit world. From these teachings we can have a hopeful frame of reference to aid in this life by removing the fears of loneliness and death. We are never totally alone in the next world, and there is no death.

In my previous book, *Darkness into Light,* I discussed rescue work where we are able to help souls who have trapped themselves in the astral plane. These souls have died, but have been unable to make their transition to the spirit world to continue their spiritual growth. An extract or review of this work is also repeated in this book. I have included an update of the subject of rescue work, as it is the source of much information about the transition process.

Each chapter of the book stands alone and can be used as a lecture series or as a class outline for teachers. Consequently, there is some repetition of some statements such as "There is no death" and "We create our own reality." Repetition where the text requires it preserves the integrity of the chapter.

CHAPTER ONE

WHY WE COME TO PLANET EARTH

As WE TRAVEL THROUGH THIS LIFE, regardless of our religious and other philosophical training, we may stop and ask such questions as: "Who am I?"

"Is there a purpose to our life on this planet?" and

"Why did we choose to come here to the earth plane?" Also,

"Where did we come from originally?" and,

"Are we a part of some divine plan?"

Much is written in our great books, like the Bible, as to why we came here. However, books are only a person's ideas of what is truth, and many changes have taken place since the books were written. They have often been rewritten by people who have changed them to reflect the ideas and times of the ones doing the revisions.

Scientists have determined that the planet has gone through many changes since the "Big Bang" projected it to the orbit around the sun, thus making it possible for human and other life forms to survive here. The planet is still changing, and continents are moving slowly to new positions. Mountains erupt or explode, and islands appear and disappear.

All life forms on the planet have developed and have adapted to the changing environment. They are in a state of constant change, and there seems to be no end to the versatility of nature.

Since mankind has been here upon this earth plane, it has advanced in intelligence, and the human body has changed greatly.

Survival was the primary physical need for man in those early days, and social life developed slowly. They did not question why they were here, and they did not seek the religious knowledge upon this plane that we now seek.

Those that were here first knew there was a force greater than they, but they did not know exactly what it was. They endowed trees, mountains, and natural phenomena, such as the weather or certain objects, with mysterious powers and worshipped them. As man's intelligence has developed, so has his need for knowledge of the truth.

There is considerable evidence that human life began on another plane of consciousness. Mankind is a recent arrival on the earth, but evidence of other life forms show that the earth was here and inhabited for millions of years before mankind arrived. There is also evidence that we live many lives on this planet, and we are seeking self-fulfillment each time we come here.

Some children are born with a strongly developed character, and many children are born with abilities that they could not possibly have learned in the time they have been here. Many people have had out-of-body experiences and report that there is a light that seems to have the power to create All That Is. People have found they could have life experiences in their dreams without a physical body, and they had faculties with greater flexibility than the ones they have on the earth plane.

We apparently have an existence in other levels of consciousness. The dream state and other out-of-body experiences, when the body is asleep, are examples of this.

Some mystics declare that we begin life as a spark of light which has a creative power and which can take on any form we wish. This energy creates the human body and it is used by the human spirit to experience life in this dimension. This physical form that we have on the earth plane is unique to this dimension.

When we come here to the earth plane, we have chosen to do so. When we return to the next plane of existence, we naturally bring memories of this physical body with us for the purpose of recognition. There we meet other people who have also been in physical form with us at one time or another. Therefore, it is easier for us to be recognized by this familiar human form. If we incarnate again, we do not take this form but assume the form appropriate to the culture and environmental conditions into which we are being born.

As we progress on different planes and go on other missions or incarnations, as we call them, we will learn that each life is part of our whole being. Our whole being includes all the knowledge gained from experiences we have had in all the earlier missions. However, each being that we have assumed in other incarnations still exists in the spirit world. When we return to the spirit world, we go through many levels of experience and eventually reach the level where we will be able to meet these other facets of our total being.

There are many different missions that we take, one of them being our life here upon this plane now. As we are a composite being at all times, the facet that is the person projected on to the earth plane at this time appears to be unique and individual.

As we come to this planet, we come as an energy form. We may have been here before, we may not have. That was our choice, and we may choose to return as many times as we wish.

We sometimes have a mission we wish to fulfill. Sometimes we come because we wish to learn things about this plane. Everything that we have chosen, both on this side and on that other side, and the way we live this life, is of our own choosing.

We chose our path in the spirit world, and then came here with a mission to fulfill. It is as if we are soldiers coming to serve here. It is not like a war upon the earth plane, but it is a struggle between right and wrong, waged within our own soul. The winner of this struggle is always our inner self.

No matter what we choose upon this earth, it is always the right choice, because it is the right one for us. We have made that choice for a reason. We know the situation that we are born into beforehand. However, once we reach the earth plane, we are free to change, and we can make decisions here, even changes in the original plan or mission.

Did we not choose the partner that we married and the house that we live in? Did we not choose the things that are in that house? Yes, we did. We chose our job and many other things, even the family situation we are in.

There are some things we may say we did not choose, but we chose the parents that we have, before we came here. We knew that choice would bring influences that were not freely chosen but were for our growth, and the growth of our parents. Again, we choose whether we will follow our parents' directions.

We have come here to learn many lessons. We may have come here to help others. We may have come here for our personal growth, or we may have come here to serve God.

All our experiences here are taken back to some other plane and added to the whole self. We must experience many things, and we can do that upon the earth plane much faster than we can in the spirit world.

The apparent reality of the physical world is a given, and life here is a challenge. Growth is accomplished by outgrowing or overcoming the challenges.

In the spirit world our thoughts manifest instantly, and as we create our own reality, there are no restrictions or challenges to overcome. Therefore, this earth is a very exclusive learning ground for anyone to develop the whole self.

We are free to choose new experiences when we come to the earth plane, even if we did not choose them before we came. We are also free to choose when we are done with this plane and we wish to return to the spirit world.

However, if we decide at an earlier time that we do not wish to complete this mission, we are allowed to stop. We can give up this life and return to the other side, where we may choose some other approach to accomplish our goal.

If there is a reason that we chose to leave, then from the other side, we will decide for ourself why we made that decision. We will be allowed to find some other means to accomplish our goals, and this may entail reincarnation to the earth plane.

We are never penalized for anything that we do upon this earth plane. We are never penalized for any decision because that decision was ours. Everyone's path to enlightenment is unique. We have to live with who we are, wherever we are.

If we wish, we can come back here and experience a previous life again to change it. However, we would have no knowledge that we are reliving an experience. Perhaps the whole experience was just a lesson for us to learn.

There are those who wish to come back time and time again, if they had experiences they greatly enjoyed. They may have been in a situation where they did things to help others, and they may have enjoyed a life without many challenges. There are also those who have come from other dimensions only to give love and service to others.

So, when we see someone here who is very successful and much loved by others, it may be they may have already accomplished what they came here to achieve. It is difficult to assess the truth of another person's quest when we base it on the façade shown to the world.

There are many different paths we can take and many different lives we may have here upon this plane. Our coming here was an act of free will, and we may come here many, many times. The term, "There is no death," does have meaning, but would eternal life on the earth plane and the merry-go-round of birth and death have any purpose or meaning?

There are many theories regarding what happens after we have completed the many trips we make to the earth plane. There are many different opinions from people in the spirit world. It is doubtful if anyone on this earth can know the truth of ultimate existence. One theory suggests we are absorbed into a God force, but it is difficult for us to know what it would be like. We cannot know what it is like to not be. To be conscious of anything means that we have life, identity, and knowingness.

I must confess I have no knowledge of what kind of existence a being has who has never incarnated into the earth plane. The questions of what they do, and what form they take, probably has to remain until we get home to the spirit world.

A life of perfect peace and tranquility, without any purpose or reason, seems boring to my earthly mind.

CHAPTER TWO

WHEN DO I BECOME ME?

W E HAVE ALREADY CHOSEN OUR PARENTS and decided the purpose of this mission when we begin the process of coming to the earth plane. We may have chosen parents that we have been with in other incarnations, in different relationships. Or, they may be strangers to us, but they live in conditions that are desirable for us to fulfill our mission. Environmental factors and other personal physical conditions have been carefully selected to provide the optimum situation for us.

We may come here with only one mission to fulfill in this particular lifetime, or we may have several. Having several missions could account for someone who has many changes in his life and does not seem to settle on any one thing.

One of the conditions taken into consideration is the question of when we enter this life. On the earth plane there is much emotional controversy regarding birth control, abortion, right to life, and free choice. The arguments seem to revolve around the question of when does life begin. As there is never a time when life does not exist, the question is really moot. From the moment of conception to the time of death, life exists here.

The point of initial contact with this dimension is not important. Whether it is when we are within the womb of the woman who is to bear us, or that we are there at conception, or at the moment of birth, are merely descriptions of various stages in the birth process. To try and pinpoint the exact moment of the beginning of life is a futile exercise. There is no death, there is only life eternal.

As far as people on the earth are concerned, the most common belief is that life begins at the point of conception, or with the birth of the child.

We are wherever we direct our attention. We identify with a particular vibration and this creates a life in that dimension. The earth plane is only one of many levels of consciousness, and we have decided to accept the limitations of the earth plane.

We can become a being whenever we choose, as long as the conditions are appropriate for us. If we have been attached to our parents from another lifetime, we will probably conform to their needs concerning the time to rejoin them and incarnate.

We may wish to come completely at the moment of conception, or we may make an initial contact, then continue to have things to finish in the astral plane. This second situation is an unusual occurrence and can lead to a child being stillborn. The entire birth situation is delicate and threatening for the incoming spirit.

Every situation that we encounter when coming to this earth plane is a matter of choice for us. We may even come directly from a higher level of existence and bring a more advanced level of spiritual contact to the earth plane.

We would still have a link to that higher level, and we can choose not to come completely into this life until things are ready for us. It is just a spark of our whole being that comes to each mission.

If we have something we wish to accomplish on the other side that is not quite finished, and it is necessary for this to be completed, then we can be what we might term, bi-located.

To be bi-located is to be aware of two levels of beingness at the same time, for example, when we know we are dreaming. In the dream we have a body that is a duplicate of the one we have left on the bed, and we are conscious of the fact that we are also alive on earth. Another example is when we see a vision of another state of consciousness. We know we are awake, yet we see another universe.

Similarly, a person in spirit can be aware of being part of the birth process and still be partially in spirit.

Whenever we enter into a limited realm such as the earth plane, we are restricted as to the amount of spiritual power we can bring. Within this limitation we can come fully into life here, especially if we know the parents we are adopting are from a previous life we have shared. In that situation there would be a joyous reunion, and the love would be carried into the earth life.

We come here with a mission, and we hope we have chosen the right circumstances for our birth to accomplish this mission. Sometimes in our eagerness to incarnate, we may pick a more difficult time to accomplish our goal and may find some problems. This may be a reason that some people are very unsettled in this life.

When we identify with the earth conditions, we take on the influences of those who have come here on this planet before us. We have to accept the earthly emotions and forget the conditions of the other dimensions. We are born with a clean sheet and are usually unaware of previous attachments.

There are exceptional cases of previous memory, but generally these memories are dormant until we re-enter the spirit world. Some people make the choice to only come here and lightly touch the earth to experience the birth process. Most of the time they do not stay longer than about three days. They may wish to establish an earthly link because they have not been here before. They will come here in the future and fulfill whatever purpose is planned. In this way they have established a link with the earth for themselves to make the contact.

Many times a person comes here to this plane and then decides he does not wish to stay. He can then withdraw and return to spirit. Remember, it is a matter of our choice whether we stay or not. We are free to change our mind at any time. We may realize that the mission we wished to accomplish may be available elsewhere. Therefore, we can change our mind and leave. There are many things that influence our decision whether we will stay here or not. We need to realize that everything is a matter of choice, and it is also a choice when we come here for the earth plane experience.

Because of the limitations imposed on us by entering the third dimension, we forget that we are eternal and immortal.

There is never a time when we are not alive and conscious in some level of vibration. This understanding will come when we leave this plane and return to spirit. The reason for many occurrences will be explained, and many differences will be resolved when the reasons are understood.

Many people here on earth spend a lot of time and energy hating other people's choices. Violent people can find an excuse to exercise their hatred under the guise of righteousness. Clinics are bombed, doctors are harassed, and clinic personnel are murdered by some self-righteous people who have a narrow view of life and wrongfully judge others. Many women have been victimized because of their choice to exercise what they choose to do with their free will and their own bodies.

Sometimes a being in spirit will lightly touch the earth to establish a contact with the earth vibration. A person on earth who wishes the experience of childbirth will volunteer in the spirit world, during the sleep state, to conceive the child, knowing it will be a short-term pregnancy.

This brief contact will enable the being from spirit to understand the earth-plane conditions. This being then will be able to be a guide to someone on the earth plane. The people involved with the child will all experience various emotions and will receive personal growth resulting from the situation.

It is only natural that we would become attached to a child born into the family, and that the loss of the physical presence would be devastating. It is only when we return to the spirit world that full understanding comes. There is tremendous emotional growth arising from the loss of any family member.

If man could realize there is no death and that this life is merely the direction our perception is focussed for a brief period, there would be less unhappiness on earth.

CHAPTER THREE

THE WHOLE BEING

WE HAVE COME TO THIS DIMENSION in the form of a small spark of light we call the God force, or the great force, or any of the different names that have been given to this totality of all that is. It is as if a ray of divine light is projected through various levels of consciousness and is resting temporarily in this third dimension.

This great creative force exists beyond anything that we on earth could possibly imagine. It is a great movement of energy which is the basis of all consciousness. We have come to the earth plane and have developed a human form and a brain here with which to create an individual personality.

We also exist on other levels, but we do not need to have a physical brain there as we do here, and yet we are fully capable of thinking and communicating with those around us. It is difficult for us to imagine how we can think, and know the past, present, and future without a physical brain. It is as if the energy itself is a creative expression. It is sensing and knowing on a different level, not thinking as we do here on this plane with a human brain.

We are energy, and we move with this energy. Everything that we do is done through this energy. Thus, we are here as an energy system that is thinking on the level of the physical world. On all other levels we do not need a physical body because we leave it here when we go to other dimensions. So we need to understand that we exist here as a bundle of energy taking human form.

All this movement takes place through the spark of being that began on a higher level. This energy, that is constantly moving, creates within itself the individual being that we are. This beingness is also part of the whole self. This whole beingness is what we know as consciousness.

This creative essence has the ability to think, to speak, to reason, yet it does not have a physical brain. When we take form at other levels, there is a knowingness that makes verbal communication unnecessary. In the spirit world we use words during the transference of thoughts until we are versed in the use of the new powers. Then we dispense with languages.

Most communication from spirit is in the form of concepts, and the mind of the medium translates the concept into words. This is how messages from spirit people of other languages can send messages through to us, even if the medium does not know the language.

In the next level of consciousness we can create an image or reproduction of ourselves, if we wish to do so. It is created as a thought-form which we recall from our memory. It needs no effort to do the recall, because it is our spontaneous idea of how we normally think of ourselves.

Sometimes a sick person will recreate himself as if he is still sick on the astral plane, but a simple change of perception remedies his self-concept.

One of the pleasures of rescue work is to make the sick person realize the spirit is perfectly healthy, and they can be any age they wish by that simple change of perception.

If we were to meet someone here on the earth plane, we might recognize them by their physical features. If we were to meet someone on another level of existence, then we would recognize them by their vibration of energy. Every person has a different aura about them, and we would recognize each person by the variations in the auric colors or the intensity of their light.

Some people in spirit choose to form their personal energy in a way that resembles a protective shield of light, and they exist within that shield. Yet when anyone comes to spirit and sees them, they would immediately be recognized because of their vibration, no matter what form they take in this first level away from the earth plane; they cannot hide.

We have within ourselves, in our auric field, our own energy vibration. It is the individual self that we have brought from the whole being in spirit that exists now within this auric field.

All of our memories exist in spirit, and that is why it is easy for us to recognize people when we meet on other planes.

Some people expect to find some form of record system in spirit. Our personal memory bank is in the form of an electrical vibration within us which we can recall. A memory bank seems unnecessary as we are part of all that is. Our minds can access any part of all that is by deep concentration or meditation. There is not some form of library as we know it on earth.

From the earth plane, we have the ability to observe what is happening on the astral plane by the use of our psychic senses. However, when people from the astral come to observe us here, they do not see the physical body, they observe only our auric field and our astral body. Spirit people can be aware of the whole spirit being, but not the individualized physical form, unless they assume human conditions.

When we arrive in the spirit world, our love for those we were close to on the earth plane becomes so pure that it creates a feeling of protection. We will come as close as we can to protect our loved ones in any way that we are able. We will be able to detect their feelings, and the guides will show us how we can send love to them, which is the greatest protection of all.

From the next level, if we come to nurture and protect others, what we have for them is pure love, non-judgmental love. Previously we had personal, possessive love which is transitory.

We judge everyone on this earth, even though we may think we do not. When we cross over, we lose this possessive love and all the ties we had. We no longer have those emotions because we no longer exist in this human form. So when we return to observe our loved ones, we do so to bring pure love and protection.

There are many people who think they can sense their loved ones around them, and this is quite possible. But do not think that spirit people can know everything that we are thinking or doing. They can receive the thoughts that we direct to them personally, because we have an established link to them. It also helps if we say these thoughts aloud to those on the next plane.

It is different when we send out generalized thoughts in prayer, because we are directing them to a spiritual force, not to a particular person. So prayer is always heard.

Imagine what it would be like if those on the other side could hear every thought of every human being. It would be overwhelming for them on that level, like a million radio waves coming directly to them.

There are people who like to ask God or someone in spirit to help them in some way. There may be many in spirit who hear this plea, and they will come as a group and will bring what help they can.

We sometimes send up a prayer in jest such as, "Oh God, I wish it would stop raining!" We do not really want this help. It is only a human expression, and it is not blasphemy.

Even if we are given all the help we think we need, we may not be able to accomplish our mission in life, and that is not spirit's fault, nor is it God's fault! This is one important reason why some prayers are not answered.

People in spirit who come in answer to our prayers do not judge, and they are not able to interfere with the mission we have chosen for this incarnation. We have chosen many challenges before coming here. However, the fact that we have free will means we have the ability to change our plans to achieve self-fulfillment in our own way.

When we can understand that the whole being is the creative principle expressing itself through us, then everything falls into place and we find peace of mind.

CHAPTER FOUR

THE BIRTH PROCESS

A T THE MOMENT OF CONCEPTION, the egg and ovary make contact and physical growth begins. The incoming spirit also makes a contact at that time, but it may be only a partial contact. There will be a spark of the personality that is to come, but the spirit may not come fully into this life until later. Sometimes the incoming soul has things to complete in the spirit world before a total commitment can be made.

During the period of incubation in the womb, there is a mingling of the auras of the incoming spirit and the mother. The mother will feel the added energy and the spiritual power brought from a higher level of consciousness. She will exhibit a glow of light and energy around her and may be emotionally stimulated throughout the pregnancy.

The mother may have some extraordinary psychic experiences and feel the wonder of the birth process during pregnancy. The child-to-be has come from a higher state of consciousness and has brought spiritual love, which is a natural state in the higher realm. There is often a sense of peace as well as excitement as she feels the fetus stirring within her.

At the time of the actual birth, the incoming soul will have time to enter completely into the physical world. As the auric fields separate, there is a shock to the system of the mother. However, this is cushioned by the presence of the spirit-guides of all concerned in the delivery room. There is so much spiritual love at birth, even though the parents may seem oblivious.

The mother will feel the loss of the extra energy at this time. The child will also have to face the world and lose the security of the womb. Usually the attending staff will induce independent breathing for the infant in some way.

There is a rush as the fields are pulled apart, which may puzzle the mother, and she may have a period of depression following the birth because of the loss of the extra spiritual power. This depression is often overcome by the joy of the experience and the potential of the infant's new life.

The child brings a pure spiritual love and increased power into the process and has to tone the power down to the earth's vibration. The birth is an extremely emotional experience, and everyone in the room will have strong feelings. They will be able to feel the energy as it begins to radiate from the child as it becomes a separate individual.

There is also a surge of energy within the child as its unseen guide from the spirit world draws near to help it begin life here on earth. Guides from spirit of the mother, the infant, and those attending the birth are all helping in this process.

There is often pain associated with childbirth, but the guides are sometimes able to alleviate much of the discomfort and help with the rapid recovery of the mother.

This whole process does not lessen the joy the parents usually feel in any way. The entire event is generally very exciting for all involved.

The parents naturally wish their child to be perfectly healthy at birth. However, the incarnating person may have decided to carry a special burden during this life. This burden is something that has already been chosen before incarnation here.

Sometimes there is a disturbance during the pregnancy which has the desired affect of creating the physical conditions that are necessary. It is difficult for many people to understand that a person may have chosen to have such discomfort in this life. However, we must realize that these are earthly things that have been chosen for experience in this lifetime only. The pain felt is not something that you bring from a spiritual plane, it is only what is learned here upon this planet.

We choose everything about this life because we have free will, and it all becomes a reality in that first moment of conception. These circumstances have already been chosen by us. If I were to say that I wish to have the experience of a deformity of some kind, I would have to discuss this in the spirit world with those who are to be my parents because it is also an experience for them. These agreements are made in the spirit world, and the parents are usually unaware on the earth plane of the challenge they have accepted. They are having a learning experience also.

We may also have someone who comes here who is mentally ill. It is just that they have chosen not to be perfect compared to the average person on the earth plane. They are perfect at the soul level. The appropriate earth conditions will have been chosen for them to fulfill their chosen experience. The moment they leave the earth plane and return to the spirit world they are fully restored. They are also shown the reason for the apparent negative earth plane atmosphere, and they are able to see the results of their influence on those they affected.

Sometimes a person in spirit will retain the memory of the mental illness and declare they are sick. Then they are reminded by the helpers that there is no insanity in spirit.

There is no physical body to become sick. In spirit, sickness is an elective for those that come to the astral plane with that identity firmly implanted in their psyche.

The primary object of incarnation into this earth dimension is to provide the maximum opportunity for the soul to reach self-fulfillment in the shortest possible time.

The duration of each incarnation is predetermined, and arrangements are made to bring about suitable conditions for the end of this life and the return to the astral plane and then to the spirit world.

After a decision is made to incarnate, a person is required to be wholly within that physical body for the allotted time period. If a person has decided to come with a special burden, it is a special opportunity for those around him or her to learn. The souls upon the earth plane are not aware that they have a prior agreement and may become bitter about the conditions they find themselves in.

The bitterness could be part of the learning process also. There are so many varieties of potential growth for the people involved in this birth process, that it is a pity we need to shroud it in mystery. If we all knew, when we came here, what we are here to learn, there would not be any point in having an earth-plane experience.

People upon this earth plane may think a new soul with a deformity cannot learn anything here. However, the new soul will know what he came here for, and he will also learn much from everything and everyone around him. He is able to absorb this knowledge on a spiritual level rather than on an intellectual level. For him, it would be as though he had been on another level of life. For example, a mentally retarded person will not measure up to normal earth plane intellectual standards, and people will not realize they are learning tolerance and love. There is an exchange of love at different levels between the burdened soul and those around him. That love may not be evident here on earth, but it is registered on a spiritual level.

The veil between the planes of consciousness permits us on the earth plane to absorb knowledge and understanding, even though we are not aware of it. Many apparent differences are resolved when we return to the spirit world.

These special circumstances are an example of spiritual preconditioning that we bring to the earth experience, and there is growth through adversity. It is easy to see how all those involved can benefit from the experience.

At the level of consciousness experienced prior to birth, the soul is a complete being with knowledge of all previous incarnations. Trace elements of previous lives may become evident in the newcomer which may cause some confusion to both the child and his parents.

Generally speaking, these past recollections fade quickly as the child becomes involved in his new life. There have been many instances of past life recall, and there is nothing for the parents to be concerned about. The barrier between the levels is extremely thin, and the ability to be aware of previous lives is usually a blessing.

In the early years of life the child is still psychically sensitive and may have contacts with spirit children. One mother of an eight-year-old girl came to me and told me her daughter at age three had told her that she had seen her mother about to become very distressed because of a divorce in the near future. The child wanted to comfort her mother and to replace the love the mother was to lose.

The mother did not understand psychic matters and told the child to suppress such nonsense, which the child did. Later the mother became more aware of other states of being and wanted me to bring back the child's psychic ability. This was not possible for me. I naturally explained that the child had set a barrier between the states of awareness.

Trace elements of previous existences can often seep through the veil, especially in the early years, and should be encouraged for the future benefit of the child. Unfortunately, there is an unnecessary fear of psychic things, and much potential ability is lost.

Despite the difficulties of pregnancy and childhood, the result is a new soul to be trained and developed that may be here to make a significant mark on the earth plane.

The introduction of a new soul into the world is a truly remarkable and beautiful experience.

CHAPTER FIVE

WHAT IS REALITY?

*T*HE REAL YOU is not your body or your mind, not your
ego, nor any part of the physical senses or emotional
feelings by which we see the world around us.

The real challenge is to discover who we really are when
all the external trappings are removed and we stand alone
in the quiet of our own mind.

Our emotions, feelings, thoughts, drives, and desires
are all transitory. Yet there is a part of us that remains as if
it was an overseer of all that we perceive. This is the inner
part of ourselves that never changes, and it is referred to as
the "I AM." The I AM precedes every thought, idea, or
action that we perform. Every appraisal of the situation
around us is first recognized, then evaluated, then referred
to our subconscious to identify. If there has been previous
exposure to a similar situation, then we know how to deal
with the present experience.

If we have not had any similar experience, we do not
know how to act. So, depending on whether the situation
is a threat or not, we usually act according to our present
feeling of security or interest.

If we meditate to try to find the core of our being, we go through a series of introspective steps. We start at the physical body level, and we find the thing we are seeking is intangible. It cannot be found in any organ of the body.

The next level of our search is in the emotions. We discover we have an emotional reaction to every observation, and we find the emotions are the evaluations of the intellect.

Next, we find the intellect is a series of thoughts which we join together to make a stream of consciousness. Each thought is individual, and we find it is possible to see a tiny gap between the thoughts. If we focus on the gap between thoughts, we can enter a state of mind expansion and become aware of other levels of beingness beyond the limitations of the physical body.

If at this stage we can surrender to a trance-like state, we will see that we are part of the creative process. In the trance state we can be aware of the oneness of all things. This new awareness makes us realize there are levels of consciousness in which we can exist without a physical body. As we return to consciousness, we see that the world is our idea and we have strong affects on what we perceive.

From the depths of our inner soul, we are creating our idea of reality. We are the creator and observer of what we create. The inner soul or divine spark within us interacts with the energy field in which our conscious mind is residing. We create our version of the world-idea that we see and apply all the past knowledge we have, in support of our idea of what is reality.

The world around us seems solid and real, but we have been shown by scientists in physics and chemistry that we are really in an energy field. We are constantly projecting a psychic imprint onto this energy field. We can always return to this imprint in the future because we are creating a memory bank to give us the idea of a stable universe.

We know that no two people see the world in the same way. Two people in the same situation will have different versions of what has happened. Witnesses of an accident have proven this many times. The same is true of witnesses describing a person to the police. Our interpretations are strongly influenced by our emotions. If we have any prejudices, then they will influence our impressions of what we see.

The idea that we create our own reality by the thoughts we think is difficult to accept, unless we are prepared to delve a little deeper into the true nature of ourselves. We usually are surface thinkers and accept what appears to be real. The thought, that we contribute in small measure to the totality of all that is, seems improbable.

The thought that we are living in a world that has been created by our predecessors makes us realize that we are creating a world for those that follow us.

We worship as we have been taught and rarely question the validity of the doctrines offered by the various faiths. We elect to office the people we think will do the best job, and rarely stop to think how we are impressed by the media barrage we receive.

Some people are able to resist the temptation to follow the masses, and these people are usually considered to be rebels. These rebels remind us that there are other ways of doing things and are usually responsible for the changes we make as we progress through life.

When we explore other states of consciousness when out of the physical body, we can see how reality consists of change. Regardless of the outcome of change, we learn that we are part of the creative force that makes all things possible.

It is not possible to know the ultimate reality while we are still in a physical body. We can only know the reality of the moment, and, as it is constantly changing, we must accept our own view of what is true. Therefore, reality is in the eye of the beholder, or, we create our own reality wherever we are.

As we progress spiritually, our sense of reality changes. Each level of awareness has its limitations and conditions, and what is true on the earth plane does not necessarily apply in other states of consciousness.

A good example of this is time. In the spirit world the time sequence and order is different. One day in spirit is like twenty-five years of earth time. People in spirit are not regulated by clocks, they just take things as they come, and go on with their version of what is real. Our sense of reality at any level of consciousness is based on a collection of beliefs we have been taught from the external environment.

From the time of our birth in the third dimension, we have been instructed by the authority figures in this world. We accept the external factors and make them our own, and this becomes the basis of our belief system. There is only one ultimate truth. We are an offshoot of the divine essence. Everything else is an attachment of beliefs, a manipulation of the creative energies.

Sometimes people from the spirit world will be brought to me for help, and they will have no idea of the date and time on earth. If a person passes from the earth but fails to let go of their ideas of earth life, they can dwell in the astral level for many years of earth time, unaware of anything else.

Sometimes a couple will swear to wait for each other in the next world. If the first one to pass on stays in the astral plane waiting for his loved one, they could very easily miss each other. I always advise people to go to the light and any meeting will be very easy there.

Often a child who goes to spirit will be looking for his mother. As the earth plane is the only reality they know, they will be roaming around near their home and their parents until they can be helped.

Recently a child was brought to me from the spirit world. She had been playing in the street and was run into by a truck. She thought she was still standing on the sidewalk looking at all the activity around her dead physical body. She could not understand why her mother was crying and what the people were looking at. I quickly got her to the light of the spirit world to be cared for there.

This kind of incident clearly demonstrates the truth that we are where our attention is directed, and we create our own idea of reality based on our expectations. This child had no idea of death and she was totally focussed on the earth plane.

As to the destiny or future of life on this planet, we are part of a group consciousness consisting of the combined thoughts of all living things. It is the energy created by this group consciousness that determines the quality of life on this planet. This group consciousness has within its control the power to decide what should come in the future.

The quality of this creative life force is determined by the spirituality of the atmosphere in this dimension. If it were possible to bring all people to the understanding of the beauty of life on this planet, then self-destruction would become a thing of the past. We would never have to live in fear of some terrorist group pressing a button to destroy all living things.

However, the creative spirit force does not control our destiny here. It is really up to us to decide our own future. Since we create our own reality and have free will, it is given to us the responsibility of self-determination. If at any time there is destruction of all living things on the earth, the earth will eventually rise again.

The power will always be here to recreate life, but there would have to be a long wait for the earth to cleanse itself.

As there is no death, we would merely transfer to another level of perception, and life for each person would continue as before.

When we die, we don't go anywhere; we merely change our perception of reality. The root assumptions that give this planet durability would be transferred to another level of consciousness and life would continue. If at that time a higher power decided that this physical planet was no longer needed, then life would not reappear on this earth, at least in human form.

If it were possible to get everyone to see that life is eternal, and love is the greatest of all powers, then there would be hope for mankind. The fear-based sicknesses would disappear, and we would be able to enjoy life on earth as it is in the higher planes. It is only when we leave this stage of beingness and go to spirit that we realize that the potential of life on earth is not achieved.

When we leave this life, we are met by loved ones, or other helpers, to get acclimatized to the new situation. Then we see there are people on the earth plane who have been trying to help mankind in raising the consciousness of man.

Eventually, everyone is helped, and the hope is this, that they will bring on earth the love of spirit next time around.

CHAPTER SIX

THE NEAR-DEATH EXPERIENCE

A MAN HAS A HEART ATTACK, he stops breathing, and doctors will declare he is dead. After a moment of blackness, he finds himself floating up out of his body, and he sees the attempts to revive him. The paramedics come and pound on his chest; he tries to talk to them, but they do not hear him.

He briefly finds he is in an area of darkness, but the moment he mentally thinks, "Where am I," he finds himself moving forward towards a light. As he travels along, he realizes he is in a tunnel, and ahead of him he can see a light which gets larger and brighter as he moves closer.

Or, as one man described it, "Here comes this white light. It didn't blind me. It was just the whitest white and the total area was filled with it.... It was just like you looked out into a total universe and there was nothing but white light."

This is the common near-death experience that has been studied and written about for years. Dr. Kübler-Ross, when a psychiatrist in the Chicago General Hospital, astounded the medical profession when she wrote a book about the near-death experience (NDE) after she had studied some two hundred cases in the hospital. As a result of her work, several doctors and other researchers have continued her work and have published their results, all supporting the truth of life beyond the grave.

The stories told by people who have had this NDE had some similar elements. All the people thought they had experienced the afterlife, and this information is beginning to change the way people regard death. Many of the subjects had been met by relatives and were told that they had to return to finish some work they had to do. The work is generally of a spiritual nature, not the mundane work of earning money.

It is estimated that eight million people have had a NDE, and the surprising thing is that most of these people were not seeking spiritual enlightenment. Because of the present acceptance by some of the the medical profession, the NDE is now considered to be the most natural doorway to spiritual transformation.

When this happens to people who are not on a spiritual quest, it can be emotionally and psychologically disturbing. Some people doubt their sanity, others think they were dreaming, and all of them were shocked to realize there is another world where life continued free of a physical body.

I was once teaching a class in California entitled Spiritual Growth and Psychic Development, and one man sat at the back of the class for the first three sessions. During the third session I talked about out-of-body experiences. After the class, this man came and shook my hand and explained that he had been a helicopter pilot in Vietnam and had the following experience. His helicopter had been shot down by ground fire and he watched this helicopter fall to the ground, unaware it was his aircraft. He watched as two soldiers in a Jeep stopped and extricated a body from the plane and took it to a field hospital. He said he followed the

Jeep for some reason, and then became aware of a tremendous pull toward the hospital and he "woke up in a sea of pain."

As he was completely unaware of life after death, he never told anyone about his NDE. He thought he would be classified as crazy if he told the Army doctors what had happened, and he did not want to be discharged under a Section 8 classification as mentally unstable. He said, "I'm not sure of all the other stuff you are teaching about the next life, but you have saved my sanity, I have worried for years about what happened to me." He left the class and I have never heard from him again.

Many people reported they saw spiritual beings surrounded by light who they thought were angels. All were aware of being fully conscious, and some experienced extraordinary powers of motion. Many reported that they saw a being or figure of light and felt they were in the presence of the God of their particular religion, if they had one.

The effects of these encounters had a profound effect on the people, and many reported that they have completely changed their ideas of what is important in life. Some experienced a life review where they were able to see some previous behavior which had hurt other people. They were amazed to see how widespread were the effects of their behavior on other people, even onlookers or people not directly involved. This made them realize the effects they have on the world around them.

The life review was usually an experience where they were able to learn how they might have done things differently. There was no judgment, no sense of punishment, just a demonstration of factual experiences for their evaluation.

As a result of this experience, many changed their attitudes and became kinder, gentler beings, and they all lost any fear of death. Most NDE people wanted to stay where they were in that other world. They all felt they were in an atmosphere of pure, unconditional love and peace. The more problems they had in this life, the more they wanted to stay.

Some of the subjects had sickness or poverty to return to, so who can blame them for wanting to stay in peace and security? The NDE is quite common for people who are sick and near death. People will often see loved ones around their bed, as if they are waiting for the person to join them.

Most subjects felt emotionally different when they returned. Anger and fear were understood as being unnecessary reactions, and they felt that anger was a waste of energy. For some there was a sense of isolation when they returned, and some changed radically and went to other jobs, often to jobs with service to others, such as nursing. The divorce rate of these subjects was higher than average, and this seemed to relate to the sense of a new life. Some people were depressed after they realized they had been asked to leave heaven and come back to this life.

To Spiritualists there is nothing new in the NDE. They are often aware of the closeness of the next world, and communication with loved ones is part of their doctrine or beliefs. To some extent, I think we have all had experiences that seem to substantiate the findings of the NDE people. I think the fact that this information is coming from doctors and scientists is making it credible. Perhaps it will bring us closer to an understanding of the next life.

I do not expect that doctors and scientists will become NDE enthusiasts. However, the fact that they are now speaking out about the afterlife is encouraging.

All the people who have come forward to researchers after they have had their NDE have not become religious, but they have become more spiritual. It's that fine line between faith and knowledge based on experience.

Some ministers who have had similar experiences have changed their teachings as much as they could without offending their congregations. Though they may accept the fact that there is an afterlife experience for many people following a traumatic shock such as a heart attack, they feel their conservative-thinking congregations would not accept such radical beliefs. Some have reported that they study the Bible for references to spirit communication and out-of-body experiences, such as Paul's revelation on the road to Damascus. He had an experience where he was unaware of which plane of consciousness he was on.

Not all doctors accept the NDE as being a spiritual experience. Some think it is hallucination or wishful thinking.

I agree it is natural for people to see what they expect to see. We take our memory with us when we go to the next life, and we get our identity from our memory of who we think we are. Our memory is full of this earth-life information and is the result of ideas and decisions we have decided to accept as being real. We structure our lives based on the result of past experience and a belief in the continuity of consciousness.

Anyone can have an out-of-body experience as a result of meditation, and we know and can prove, at least to our satisfaction, that we are in touch with higher levels of consciousness. Drug-users have reported similar experiences, but their descriptions can be discounted because of their lack of consciousness during the episode.

Of course, if an atheist accepted the fact that it is a spiritual experience, he would lose any credibility. Anyone who believes that, when we die, that's the end of it all, has to refuse to accept the teachings of some of our greatest thinkers. I have found that people who spend their life debunking spiritual and psychic phenomena cannot suddenly accept such a reversal of ideas.

The NDE experience is profound for those who have an open mind, and the result is usually a spiritual uplift for them. They are quite convinced they have seen the next life, and many are looking forward to going back when it is their time.

If you are fortunate to be talking to someone who has recently had an NDE, be careful not to assume that they now know much about the next life. The NDE may be their first out-of-body experience, and it may have confounded them. Their previous religious values may have been turned upside down, and they may need to be just listened to. Let them lead the discussion until they begin to ask questions, then you can share things based on your own spiritual experiences.

We do not have to wait for a NDE to discover the next life. We can meditate and discover for ourselves that we can extend our sensitivity to include the next dimension. There we will find a universe of peace and serenity once we have let go of this plane. When it is your turn to make a transfer to the next life, you will have no trouble, because you will have an expectation of meeting loved ones.

So go to the light when you make the change, and they will be waiting for you.

CHAPTER SEVEN

CROSSING OVER TO SPIRIT

*T*HERE SEEMS TO BE SOME CONFUSION here on the earth plane concerning what to expect when we die and leave this world. The first problem that most people have is realizing that there is a next life. Then they have to realize the next life is a continuation of this one and only our perception of what is real changes. All previous belief systems have to be reviewed and most of them dropped. The process of letting go begins as soon as we realize we are in a new world.

We can access this next life and obtain information to verify its existence in many ways.

The first, and the most obvious way, is when we die and our spirit is released to the next world. We separate from the physical body and find we are in a duplicate body which seems as real as the physical one we have left behind. We discover we can change this spirit body and assume whatever form we like by changing our self-perception. In spirit we have faculties that are better than the earthly ones, and we have extra mental powers that we have to learn how to use and control.

Second, is the natural experience of dreams. We enter the dream world when we sleep. We have opportunities to explore this sleep state, and we find we have powers that allow us to pass through obstacles. We also have the ability to change our location by a simple change of perception.

We find we are, where we think we are, because the image-creating ability of the mind manifests our thoughts.

During this past life we have made connections with many people, some positive, and some negative. With each connection we automatically establish lines of communication.

We establish special links between our loved ones and ourselves, and we can use these links to meet those who have passed to the next life. The positive links are joyful reunions, and the negative links need a little work to resolve any misunderstandings. We need to learn that each link is a necessary part of our growth plan, and the total self, or whole being, is outgrowing unnecessary emotions and belief systems.

Third, is to learn how to meditate and find some way to extend the sensitivity of our consciousness to include visions of some of the next levels of awareness. This meditative process can be easily learned and can be done in private. There is plenty of good literature on the subject, and there are many teachers and study groups available. Most groups are open to anyone seeking to broaden his experience to include some explanations of the next world.

I have three golden rules that I pass on to all my students regarding group meditation.

1. Let common sense be your guide. If it sounds too good to be true, it probably is.
2. Keep your feet firmly on the ground. Don't become so heavenly that you are no earthly good. Remember you are here for the purpose of spiritual growth, through experience of the earth plane.
3. Let your money be the last thing you part with. Be careful. We read of many situations where people are

swindled of all their money by unscrupulous people promising enlightenment.

The object of meditation is to experience a shift of our focus from this world to some other dimension. The first thing to be kept in mind is that there are many levels or planes of awareness that can be experienced. There are many conflicting reports about the requirements necessary to have extra-sensory-perception, or an out-of-body-experience. I can assure you that you do not need to leave your home. You do not need to join an organization or go to a "holy" mountain to find the truth of survival of the human spirit after death.

Some people refer to the astral plane as the spirit world, but the astral level is really an extension of the earth plane. It is not regarded by spirit people as a level of the spirit world. However, names and titles of consciousness levels are not important; they are only useful as reference points.

The astral plane is so close to this earth plane that we slip into it whenever we sleep. Even when we daydream or have periods of deep reverie, we are partially withdrawn from this world and are on the fringe of the astral plane. We still replicate our physical body and are still locked in to a time sequence similar to earth time.

There are many different planes or levels of awareness that are accessible to the seeker. We automatically go to the level of awareness that we are compatible with, so we all go to our heaven. Consequently, it is difficult to know exactly which picture of reality any one person will experience in these other dimensions. There are different reports by many people who have had a near-death-experience or other examples of psychic out-of-body experience. Each experience will be true for that person.

As we create our own reality and we react individually to any environment we find ourselves in, we all go to the level we expect to find when we leave this dimension.

We must have the understanding that there is no death, and those of our loved ones who have died on the earth plane are very much alive on the astral plane. Generally speaking, they will be there to meet us when we go to join them or to visit them.

During the meditative process, we may experience visions of people who have died, and we may be able to converse with them telepathically. We may be able to bring back recollections of beautiful scenes and magnificent colors. These experiences are diversions from the true purpose of meditation, which is to find our true self. However, they are enjoyable diversions and are evidence of the existence of the next world.

The people who come to meet us will all be people we have known in the past. Some of them we will recognize, some we will not. Remember, we will be looking for those who are from this recent life, and there will be some we do not remember immediately because they come from other incarnations. But as people come forward to introduce themselves, then there will be instant recognition.

This interaction with people from other lives awakens activity within the soul where there is a remembrance of all there has been in the past. We have an opportunity to review previous lives and meet other aspects of our higher self. This can be an enlightening experience.

There are many surprises for us when we make the transition to spirit. We learn that we have always had many psychic and spiritual powers which we could have used if only we knew how.

For example, we all have an aura around us which is an energy field created partly from within us and partly from the spirit world. It is active on both the physical and the astral planes and is the magnetic energy field through which we can sometimes experience things intuitively.

The aura created by our experiences on the physical plane will blend into all other extensions of our selves at all levels and will become part of the soul memory.

Similarly, whenever we project into the astral plane, the meeting of our aura with the aura of another soul allows us to communicate with them without words. There is a telepathic knowingness shared by both parties.

The aura radiates a bright light which indicates the spiritual level achieved through the soul's growth. It becomes brighter as we clean out each negative thought or inhibition that prevents us from being a completely loving person. The brightness is an indication of our level of spirituality.

What I have been talking about is spiritual growth. Some things will be new to us, and some objects, such as flowers, will seem so much brighter. They radiate color from within themselves and do not need the reflected rays of a sun.

We may also see beings of light. As we approach them, we see how our own aura brightens and we feel the love they have for all beings. The same thing happens when we see a loved one on the astral plane, or on earth. Both auras brighten considerably because of the love being exchanged. This emotional exchange negates the need for words to a great extent. We think of it as a feeling of friendliness, but things are happening at other levels.

The main thing we will all notice is the love that surrounds those who come to meet us. There is a feeling that we are able to open up when we meet with them.

It is merely a vibration change as we go from one level to another, but there is a wonderful feeling of freedom as we approach people on the other side of the veil and feel the love they project.

One thing that seems obvious is that some of the people

we meet have a brighter aura than others. Those with the brighter aura have a stronger force of love emanating from them, and there is a wonderful feeling of acceptance of them and by them.

Eventually, we come to the realization that we on earth are also a representation of our higher self. Then the reality hits us that the figure we exhibit on earth is a projection from our soul into the earth's energy field. There may be times during our development when we can see our physical body lying on the bed where we left it. Yet the body we are exhibiting in the astral plane looks identical to the one we have left behind. This is one of those illuminating moments when our whole idea of reality changes. In the past we have thought of the world as being out there, and we are in a dualistic state. Now we see that the world is our idea and it is an internal creation.

This chapter is a brief summary or review of what happens when we have a shift in consciousness to the astral plane while we are alive on earth.

Of course, things are much clearer when we have separated entirely from the earth plane, but enough can be learned during astral projection or dreams to give us a good idea of what to expect when we die.

This earth life is very important to our growth, and a balance between the two life experiences is desirable. Try to see the world as the result of the same force that created us all, and this life will be more beautiful than we ever imagined.

So give unto spirit a daily exercise in meditation, but remember you are a human being and are here for a purpose and have acquired responsibilities for your personal growth.

The daily exercise in meditation will reinforce our spirituality, and the love that we will achieve will strengthen our faith in the divine spark within us.

CHAPTER EIGHT

TO BE A PERSON

*I*N ORDER TO EXPRESS OURSELVES IN ANY WAY, we must use our personality. This is the facade we present to the world. We create our personality by interaction with the environment. It is the sum total of our response to all experiences, both here and in spirit. It includes the ego by which we determine who we think we are on this planet.

The ego looks out mainly into the third dimension and acts as a channel for the creative powers of the inner self. The personality has strong connections to the inner or higher self and is the part of us that survives death. So we need to understand that the personality has no limitations apart from those that we accept. There is no limit to its perception. There are no boundaries except those that we create and perpetuate. There is no veil through which the human mind cannot penetrate, except for the cloud of unknowing.

The Cloud of Unknowing is a phrase used by Thomas Aquinas. He said: "If we try to see God we are confronted by a cloud or veil which separates us from other levels of experience, and we must use meditation on the love of God to reveal the truth that sets us free." He was a mystic in the thirteenth century who seemed to know what he was talking about.

He believed there are two kinds of knowledge, revelation and philosophy. Revelation is from the higher forces, and philosophy is the science of reason.

When we try to meditate, we are met by this veil or barrier. For years I was confronted by a blackness through which I could not penetrate. One day I decided to stop trying and just accept the limitation. My teacher assured me it can be penetrated by surrendering to the power of the higher self. He said we do this every time we experience a consciousness shift to the next plane, even when we sleep. I persevered and eventually I had success.

My first mystical experience came one day during my daily meditation. I decided that I had to know what was on the other side of that barrier. I thought that I would rather die than not know. Suddenly, I went through the veil into the most beautiful golden light. Apparently, it took the total surrender of the ego to achieve the breakthrough.

Somehow, I knew I was in the midst of the basic stuff of the universe. It seemed to be pure, vibrant energy. That experience brought a personality change in me, and I knew I had seen the creative forces of the universe. As I experienced the oneness around me, I knew I had to be still. The moment I had a thought, which happened to be of a chair, it materialized and the most beautiful chair appeared.

I soon learned that I could not achieve the higher states of consciousness when I liked. For the next year or so I had many spontaneous mystical experiences, and I learned much of the nature of the universe and the other states of awareness.

These are fleeting moments when we are able to be in those levels of awareness, but they are sufficient to let us know of the existence of these higher planes and the wonders of the inner universes. Without these moments, we would never know there is something at the end of our spiritual quest.

I knew that I had found the core of my beingness. I knew the truths I had discovered would never be forgotten, and I had a knowingness about the creative process. However, I still had to live in this world, which I had once seen as a spectacle of variations of light density. I wondered why I was having these experiences, so I went to my teacher in spirit, who said, "My son, you were permitted those experiences so that you could teach with conviction, not belief."

The next experiences involved a number of out-of-body exploits. Each night I would leave the body and explore the inner planes. Throughout this whole period I felt my personality was being molded, and I was reluctant to surrender completely to the desire to know myself.

I discovered that the personality, because of its link with the higher self, has access to all levels of consciousness, and these can be accessed by meditation. Consequently, the personality has great power and appears to be unlimited in its capabilities. It creates the ego and has to give the ego free choice. Regardless of the level of thought in which we are expressing ourselves, we have our own individuality which allows us to experience where we are. The conscious mind is also one of its functions.

The conscious mind is obviously very important. It allows us to maintain awareness of our daily life here on earth. It also allows us to shut out influences from the spirit world. This is unfortunate, for it is of great value for us to see into those other levels of consciousness normally screened from us.

One of the most enlightening things that I discovered is that we are not at the mercy of some spirit entity or other spiritual influences. However, we can, and should ask for help in reaching the truth about ourselves. We are not puppets on a string. There is not some super-being who deals out pain and suffering, or rewards us for being good.

If we do not like the life we have created for ourselves, all we have to do is to raise our thoughts and our expectations. We must change the messages we are sending to our bodies, to the world around us, and especially to our friends in spirit. They follow our ideas and try to help us materialize them. Each thought we have obviously has a result on the earth plane through our sense of self.

Any thought we have seems to arise spontaneously and it seems to follow our desires. Such thoughts, repeated often enough, will appear to have a more permanent reality. This is creativity in action. We create our own reality by the thoughts we think. I cannot repeat this often enough. If this is not understood, if we do not keep ourselves open for change and growth, then wrong thoughts become real and we are stuck with an incorrect idea of reality.

The one message that comes to us loud and clear from the spirit world is that the creative force, that we call the infinite, is in all things, and this divine essence is love waiting to manifest through us. All we have to do is express it.

Remember that anything we do is our choice, and as such we are expressing our desires and free will. Man is constantly growing and changing and ultimately will make the right decisions for himself and for the good of the planet.

Some people become the victims of incorrect ideas about reality and find life unbearable. Such problems as anxiety and depression are rampant in today's society and people attach themselves to fearful ideas. The secret of life is that love abounds. Many people have lost sight of this truth. Salvation is not outside of ourselves, but is obtained by self-acceptance and the realization that there is a divine spark within us that is a direct link to our own higher self.

"Seek and ye shall find, for the kingdom of heaven is within," said the Master Christian.

Spiritual people and mystics are ahead of the game in that they know there is no such thing as death, and we will continue to be active and growing in other levels of being. All we can do here is to try and make the place better for our having been here, and that means service to mankind in God's name.

CHAPTER NINE

SPIRITUAL AWAKENING

MANY PEOPLE SPEND THEIR LIVES in pursuit of material things and think little of the spiritual aspects of life. To them, material things are indicative of success. However, there are moments in the course of a life when there are optimal conditions for spiritual growth and material possessions are of no help.

When something happens that upsets our idea of who we are and how everything is, there is an opportunity for spiritual growth. We are open then to sudden change. The realization that there are times when we are powerless is a sobering thought, and this can be a time of spiritual progression for a person. When there is a life-threatening situation such as a tornado, many people will raise their thoughts in prayer and be open to spiritual awakening.

An example of spontaneous mystical experience can occur when there is the descent of grace during meditation. When this happens, it can trigger the awakening of the spirit within.

It is usually experienced as a brilliant light and a surge of power that comes from above the head and sweeps down through the body. It seems to permeate every cell and there is a cleansing feeling. It appears to realign or renew the physical body, and it feels as though we are temporarily transported to another dimension. Suddenly, the realization comes to us that everything is composed of one force, and we are part of it, and everything is where and how it should be.

I once had a student who was in a car wreck. The car was totaled but she was completely untouched. From the moment of the wreck, she was in an elevated state of consciousness in which she saw everyone emanating nothing but love and light from within.

She had withdrawn from this level of consciousness following the shock of the collision, and entered a higher state of perception. This state lasted for about a week and then she began to regain her previous mind set. We cannot live at that level in this world for long.

When something like that happens, whether we will look for a quick means to close the protective screen we surround ourselves with, or whether we change, depends on the spiritual knowledge we have at that time.

This is a signal for a massive life change when you know you are never going back again to the life you have known. This is the time to find peace within and accept the upcoming changes.

Under most conditions, the model we have of who we are seems to be stable. The world seems solid, but when a big change threatens, some people begin to fall apart and panic. We fear the loss of sanity and often mistake spiritual experiences for hallucination.

Just prior to passing, a person may see loved ones from spirit around their bed and know that they have come to reassure him or her that they will be there to meet them. This seems to be similar to the kind of experience a person has at the approach of death. For instance, imagine a person lying in bed with a terminal illness and knowing they are in that bed for the duration of their life. They may see some possession of theirs they can never use again, such as a car, or a closet full of clothes they know they will never wear again.

Care-givers and loved ones will have a different attitude when they attend to their needs, and they know the patient is dying.

These are examples of the breakdown of recognizable life systems, such as the intellectual defenses and the structure of one's self as a psychological being.

The loss of self-control and mastery of one's own life means we are losing our individuality or identity. This can be a frightening experience.

If you happen to be with someone at the time of their passing, and the person is conscious and lucid, they may be ready for spiritual awakening. This is the time to help them find God. Look for opportunities to separate yourself from the emotional dilemma and help the person find their true self. Reassure the person of the survival of the human spirit. Help them to see that the body is a separate entity and is no longer useful.

If they have any ideas that God is formless or up in the sky, they have been misinformed, because at this moment you should both know that God is there and is within you both. If the person is hanging on to this life and praying to find God, it is not going to happen. They are denying that God is within, they are saying that God is out there somewhere. Once they can accept the truth that God is within, suddenly their whole belief system about God changes and the realization of the divinity and oneness of all things becomes apparent.

We intellectually accept that statement about God being within, but we really have little idea about what that really means. If God is All That Is, then all that is, is within us, and we are projecting the whole idea of the universe from within ourselves. Can anyone in this life really understand that we create our own universe by the thoughts we think?

The process of spiritual awakening is where the inner self is separating itself from the various forms it has created. The physical body is only one of its forms. The self is recognizing that we are responsible for where we are at any particular time, and that we are an essential part of the one creative force that creates all that is. Once that realization comes, then things begin to fall into place.

For instance, you will learn that health or sickness is part of this earth life and is included in the totality of all things. It is the manifestation of the inner self and is the result of our chosen life-style here on earth. Once we return to spirit, all the earthly conditions and attachments fall away.

To the extent that we consider death as an enemy, we are stuck in our old beliefs. Life on this earth can be dangerous, but death is a perfect escape, it is not the enemy.

Encourage the person to let go and make the transition through that imaginary door into the spirit world. Help them to drop all the baggage, including the body, and get on with the process of rebirth into the next experience in the fourth dimension.

What happens next is determined by what our heart and mind and being are ready to accept as truth. Tell them not to get caught up in temptations or diversions along the way, but to move toward the light up ahead. Do not fear the change, don't push, or try to get back. Have them recognize they are dying to this world and they can continue living a new life in the spirit world.

We might advise anyone we feel is receptive to the truth of survival that there is no death, and we can keep it in mind as we progress toward the time for our own crossing.

When the time comes, we may find we are being sucked down into fear or guilt over past experiences. It's too late to change anything then, so we should just relax and let go, and just be attentive to what is going on around us. If possible, we should take care of fear before we are faced with the transition to the next life. It saves a lot of delay in getting free of this world. Just keep in mind that we are indestructible and immortal.

Some religions have made death a mystery and a place of punishment for supposed sins. In our society we feel that death is the biggest of all melodramas. We spend lots of time worrying about loved ones who are dying, and we spend lots of money on funerals when they have gone. We feel we need to show the world what good people they were by remembering them with memorials.

We talk about closure. Some people who are caught up in the illusion of the reality of this life want to inter their loved ones in an expensive coffin in a memorial garden and place some flowers around the grave site. That is their choice and this ritual probably eases the pain of separation.

These survivors of the deceased may not be ready to hear that there is no death, that the physical body in the coffin is not their loved one. It is better to continue to be sympathetic for their benefit, but know that we are playing a role. Let others have their grief period and tread lightly on their beliefs, for each person will grow at his own pace.

The one task I try to perform in rescue work is to help the deceased realize they are not dead. So many of the souls who are brought for help do not believe in survival. They are firmly convinced they are still on earth and are just a little confused with what has happened to them.

This rescue situation is a perfect opportunity for spiritual growth, and the rescue worker can help the person raise his consciousness to a higher level and find their loved ones who have progressed to the spirit world. I try to help them understand that death is a promotion not a curse.

The body is of the earth and returns to the physical energy field. The spirit is the only real thing we have and it does not hang around here long after the body has been discarded.

If there is a fear of death, we are merely transmitting our own fear onto a future event and we will have to outgrow it again. It is easier to do it now, before we get to that stage. Be open to spirit, to our guides, to our loved ones who have preceded us, and go with the flow of life that continues after this experience that we think is so real.

We have an ego that looks out into this dimension and accepts that what it sees as real. However, we have another aspect of the ego that looks in the direction of the inner self and its various levels of experience.

Sometimes I am told by those going to spirit that the light is too bright for them to accept. I tell them to relax and focus their attention on the light, I know they will soon adjust. When they do this for a few moments, there is a transformation that takes place in the atmosphere surrounding them. There is a consciousness raising as they accept the new dimension, and I encourage them to let the light show them where their loved ones are waiting. This always works, even if they are not keen on their relatives. Sometimes a person will say their relatives will not want to see them because of previous problems.

However, the moment they focus on the light, they have an awareness of the love and warmth that comes to them, and it seems they have to respond to it.

While we are waiting for our promotion, we might practice meditation. The journey is pleasant and spiritual growth is the reward. Practice daily and reap the benefits of love from spirit.

At any time there is a question about the things I have said, sit quietly and listen to the inner self. It is inviting us to raise our awareness to our higher self, that divine spark within. Do not base beliefs on what we have learned in this world, including the things I have said. Start to extend the sensitivity of your consciousness to discover the truth for yourself.

With this increased sensitivity will come the love and warmth that awaits us whenever we look within.

CHAPTER TEN

LIFE ON THE EARTH PLANE

*B*EFORE WE COME TO THIS PLANET for a life experience, we are in contact with those who are to be our parents. The ones that we have chosen to share this mission will be directly involved at this stage, for they must also agree to be a part of any plans we are making. Our plans will come together, and it becomes a joint venture for all concerned. Our parents will benefit from the mission and will volunteer to help us through our formative years. The interaction of family members will be emotional growth for all.

We will also need others to come with us. There are many others in spirit who are also wishing to come to the earth to accomplish a mission. If their mission coincides with ours, we can arrange circumstances to bring each person into their particular role. If we wanted to come here and experience being the victim of a crime, then we must find someone who needs the opportunity to be the criminal. The decision must be reviewed and evaluated when we get here on earth to see if we still wish to be involved in a crime. Regardless of the role we have elected, we will be able to resolve everything when we return.

If we wanted to discover some great invention, we would be given the opportunity to do so. Again, it is still a personal choice once we get here. We have chosen on the other side the major things that we wish to accomplish. However, at any time we are able to change our program. These elective changes cause some of the disturbances that families go through.

We have expectations wherever we are at any time. If decisions are made in the spirit world, and then are changed when we enter the restrictive earth plane conditions, many plans have to be rearranged. Great hopes in the spirit world often fail to materialize here on earth.

All of the major decisions, and many of the minor decisions, will be determined before we incarnate. We know before we come here what our major life choices are going to be. The plans are not cast in stone, and we are usually unaware of these goals once we enter the earth's vibration.

Very few people are fortunate enough to know what challenges have been accepted. For example; if we knew we would be killed by a car on a certain date, we would not go near a car on that day. However, circumstances seem to direct us to the point where we are faced with the necessary challenges.

We are unaware when we come here that we have one person on another plane who has chosen to be with us throughout this visit here, and is known as a guardian angel or guide. There are many names for this being and it varies in different cultures. They are there to give guidance to us if we ask for it. There are many who feel they do not want this contact, so they will not allow this other being to come close to them in order to help them.

Some people are very open and are aware of the presence of their guide and seem to be able to converse with them. Any time we raise our thoughts to a higher level, our guide will be able to detect and respond to the request. The guides will help us and are willing to do so when we ask for help through prayer or meditation. Our guide does not live his life through us. They do not direct our thinking or make decisions for us. They are able to direct influences such as love to help us.

One reason for the presence of these guides, and others from spirit, is to provide us with a direct contact back to the spirit world. Those in spirit who are helping us for this lifetime attend councils in spirit with us. It was at one of these meetings that we were given the choice to come here for the mission we wish to accomplish.

If the guide sees that we are not accomplishing our goal, or there are decisions that we are refusing to make, our guide will help us to make these decisions by bringing to us what they feel we need to know about our life here. We can contact them by meditation or in the sleep state at any time. We also have the ability to block them out. However, most of us, unknowingly, will receive guidance from them when we are sleeping or meditating. Sometimes when we wake from a dream and feel we have the answer to a problem, it is usually the result of having consulted with our guide.

When we come to the earth plane, we have chosen many things we would like to see happen. However, we are sometimes too ambitious. Fortunately, we have a choice at any time to decide that this life is too complicated for us to accomplish our goal, and we do not wish to be here any longer. Then we can return to the other plane. That is always our choice.

Similarly, we have set a time period for this incarnation, but we can change that. If we have decided that we wish to be here for a specified period and we decide at that time it is not long enough, we can choose to stay longer.

Many people do only stay the number of days that they have previously chosen. But there are many who do not for one reason or another. Something may have changed because people around us, who have come to share this life with us, have influenced our decisions. Even though we eventually make every decision for ourself about our life, we are influenced by others, and we must decide whether to accept what they are saying.

We have picked the circumstances into which we would like to be born, so we know whether we were to be born into great wealth or into poverty. At that time, we know what we wish to achieve or accomplish, but that information is usually hidden from us on the earth plane.

Some people come into a life of poverty when they wish to accomplish the feeling of a challenge. Self-fulfillment in this life is achieved by giving great love to those around us, and we may go to what we might call a simple life to achieve this. The area of greatest need provides the best opportunity for service.

A person may accomplish as much in the simple life as those who have become great leaders and made great decisions for many people. We chose our path before we came here, and we know that any accomplishment is added to our whole being, regardless of the circumstances of the life.

There is no reward or punishment for anything we do in life here, except the great satisfaction for reaching the goal we have set for ourselves. If we can achieve unconditional love, that is the greatest accomplishment of all.

The earth is an emotional plane. However, the emotions that we are experiencing here are not needed on the next planes. The negative emotions of hate and guilt are all peculiar to the earth plane. There is only one emotion that we carry from this lower plane, and that is love. Nothing else, only the awareness of love. For love is a state of consciousness and is present wherever we are. All other emotions only exist to aid in our search for fulfillment while we are on the earth plane.

If we could imagine a state of consciousness where every thought or desire is materialized instantly, we would understand why emotions have no place on the higher planes of awareness. If we see someone who is filled with hate for themselves and for others around them, we can help them by giving them love. Be aware that as they leave this plane, they may learn why they had that emotion so strongly here. They may have chosen it as an experience.

We can experience emotions to such a great degree that we can outgrow them. In this way we can learn of another person's suffering, and learn how to help them. We may choose to be a victim to help another on their path, and we would also learn from that experience.

At any time we can change our mind on the earth plane and not follow through on the master plan. For example, there may be many who are going to be on an airplane that is to crash. We may choose at the last moment, as many have, not to board that plane. We may have chosen before we came to have the experience of that crash, but then changed our mind.

We always have a choice for each decision we have made. The decisions we made before we came here have an affect on the life we have chosen. The goal we have chosen is predetermined, but not the decisions we will make when faced with the choices on how to accomplish the goal. That is where our free will comes in.

When we make a decision to leave this life, we may not wish to make contact with those who come to meet us, for one reason or another. That is our choice. However, those of us who realize a transition has been made will be met by those who love us.

Many differences will have been resolved, and previous feelings will no longer matter. We will have left the earthly emotions where they belong, on earth. After loved ones have greeted us, they will take us to a place where we can realize what we have accomplished in this life.

We do not have to do this immediately, but it will be something we may wish to do. We will be able to see if we have accomplished the goal of this lifetime, and be able to see how the decisions we made have affected the whole self.

We will see that we may have chosen many things that we wish to add to the whole self as an experience. We will see that we are progressing and developing the whole self by the experiences we have had in this incarnation.

We can also experience things on the next plane that will help us to grow while we are still on earth. Although we have greater faculties there, we are not all-knowing. The astral plane is only one small step on our long journey home.

We are on the bottom rung of a learning program here on earth and we progress from here. We grow from the experiences we have chosen and completed. Should we not experience what we set out to do on this trip, then that is right for us. Every decision we make is the right one for us. There are no wrong decisions, only experiences we do not like.

As we choose our own experiences, we have no one to judge us but ourselves. We make these choices in spirit before we are born, or on earth, in meditation, or in the sleep state. We may choose to deviate from the original plan and still arrive at the destination. We may make minor changes along the way, but the long-term goal will still be achieved.

A man may lose his parents at a very early age, and then spend a lifetime seeking love from others. He will eventually realize that this is an emotional experience he has chosen where he will seek to have love from others and not the nurturing love from his parents. We all experience loneliness at some time in this life, and that experience can make us realize we walk an individual pathway regardless of the friends we make.

We may come here wishing to set an example for others, and would dedicate our life to service. We may experience many smaller things on the way to achieving a larger goal. During the journey, we are flexible as to the smaller goals, but all results are reported back to the whole self.

Sometimes the great plans we make do not materialize. We may wish for something concerning another person and they may not agree. Prayer for the sick may be rejected by the patient. We do not know another person's agenda, and we can learn from the rejection.

When we leave this body and take our memory of all we have learned back to spirit, we see the reasons for the experiences we have had. We do not go to a place of darkness and judgment, we go to a place of love and enlightenment.

People who have started their transition with a near death experience and were sent back, or they changed their mind, have reported the wonderful greeting they received. They experienced an uplifting force, and felt the unconditional love from the people who came to meet them. There is a complete absence of fear and a wonderful feeling of freedom.

When we withdraw from this life, it will mean we are withdrawing our consciousness to another level. We still realize who we are, but we may not know what is happening right at that moment. Once we see those we have known upon this plane in our physical lifetime, we quickly understand there is a change in our environment and our life style. They will come in recognizable form, and our guide will be there also.

In a very short time we are met and escorted to the level of consciousness that is compatible to our spiritual achievement. There is absolutely nothing to fear. A lot of incorrect information is given out by those that do not know the truth. Many people get their information from the television horror stories.

There is nothing but love and kindliness awaiting us when we cross over. We do not have to wait until then. We can tune in and experience the love of spirit at any time. We have only to tune in to the higher state of awareness.

CHAPTER ELEVEN

TIME

*I*N THIS THIRD DIMENSION we think of time as a measurement of our awareness or consciousness when we are awake. Wakefulness is an event which arises, has duration, and passes into memory. If we sleep, we anticipate that there has been a passage of time, and we can know the amount of time that has passed by some simple arithmetic. This is known as clock time, and in the modern world most people regulate their lives by it.

We know that this clock time is where we measure the passage of time according to the movement of the seconds, minutes, and hours on a clock face. We set our clocks to coincide with instruments at the Greenwich Observatory in London, and we have worked out a system whereby every place in the world conforms according to their geographical position. Navigation systems are based on clock time, and this is an important factor when a ship needs to know its position at sea. This works well, and we can enjoy conformity so that we can fit into the scheme of things and regulate our activities. We can schedule events and set the time for these events to begin and end.

Using this system to count the passage of events, we can create history and think in terms of years and ages. We have assigned names to time periods and called them things like The Ice age, The Iron age, etc. This system locks us into a belief that this is a valid way of looking at life. This is a useful regulatory system using the clock as a guide.

However, there is also physical time. This is where we judge the passage of events by the seasons created by the rotation of our planet around the sun. There are still places where people start their day at daybreak and end it when the sun goes down. We designate names for the changes of the seasons and call them spring, summer, fall and winter. Before clock time was invented by man, this was the only recognized method of measurement of events.

There is another sense of time, an inner sense, which can be called psychological (psi) or mental time. This time varies according to our appreciation of events occurring around us. Sometimes an event will seem to drag or may seem to go by very quickly. Using psi time, we can rapidly review a long sequence of events and see things as we wish to see them.

We can imagine a trip to another country and feel we are there experiencing the atmosphere and the people. This can happen in a few minutes of psi time, but in physical time it could take days or weeks.

Any communication coming to us from the spirit side of life must come in the form of psychological time. The inner senses pass the information to the mind of the recipient, and it is transferred or translated into thoughts, feelings, ideas, and language in physical time terms.

In any out-of-body experience, we can have the passage of great periods of time in a few minutes of earth time. The body does not age the amount of time we experience in dreams because body growth is regulated by physical time and its constraints. Mental time is free of such conditions.

If we try to bring mental time events into our physical time experience, we have to recall a memory of the events.

It seems we experience an event totally, then reduce it to parts that we can understand in this third dimension. This causes some distortion of the experience, and in the transfer of this dream experience, some influence from our personal feelings may distort what we have experienced. A remembered dream is an example of an activity on another level of consciousness that does not fit our physical clock-time system.

If a clairvoyant medium is giving messages to a person and tries to interpret a symbol, he may get a different idea of the meaning of the symbol intended by the communicators. The symbol is probably a coded message between the person in spirit and the recipient on earth.

The prolific composer, Mozart, claimed he would receive a total symphony in his mind. He said it felt like a droplet of light, or as if it was in a capsule. He said it took him weeks to transfer the information to written musical form. He claimed he would have every note of each instrument very clearly in his head. Other artists have a similar experience when they are creating their particular art form. They try to reproduce a mental image to a physical reality.

Sometimes a person will receive some inspiration when in a reverie, and what seems like a new idea may be experienced. One theory suggests that an invention is introduced to the world at its appropriate time when the earth plane is ready to receive it.

I believe that many ideas come to us into this state of consciousness and are not acted upon. They are often rejected by the recipient. Many fantasies and dreams are repressed in defense of the ego when the ideas seem too remote to be true or too threatening for some reason.

The ego is a point of reference between the astral plane and the mind/brain physical reality. It is not an organ like the heart or liver; it is a free-flowing energy field that filters out information considered inappropriate for this third dimension. The ego is usually directing its attention toward the physical plane, and it often disregards anything coming from a higher vibration. Hence, we only see things in physical time and not psi time unless we are clairvoyant.

Some mystics and other gifted people are able to bypass the ego and see into the next dimension. We do this when we dream, and we can experience everything I have mentioned above when we are out of our body in the sleep state.

There is only the NOW. If we recall the past, we do so by bringing the memory of an event to the present moment. The same is true of thoughts of the future. We are projecting our belief in a future period and we do so in the NOW.

We create and use clock time to give us a past and future. We use the present moment as a point of reference on which to base our idea of beingness in this third dimension. This gives a sense of reality to life and lets us expand our sense of being into infinite periods of time. The whole thing is a mental experience in the NOW.

In the present time scheme, all things that have happened and were observed are stored as memory and are available for recall.

I have been told many times by advanced beings in the spirit world that all future events have already happened, but are in another level of consciousness. When we use our imagination, we can create the future which may or may not become a reality in this third dimension. In reality, the time divisions we use are arbitrary. In meditation we can withdraw our attention from the present moment and enter the timelessness of some higher rate of vibration.

There are states of vibration where there is just a sense of beingness, and all things are seen as one energy field. In that state of oneness there is no concept of change and, consequently, no sense of time. When we are out of our body during astral projection, we can experience a sensation of timelessness. This sensation is only known in retrospect after we have returned to this physical state of awareness.

The whole time scheme of past, present, and future is essential in this third dimension. Unfortunately, it does create a lot of confusion. On earth we think in terms of beginnings and endings, and causes and effects. These things are part of the earth plane experience only.

Many ideas related to time as we use it take on a validity which is not true in the larger design of things. Reincarnation is a good example of a belief system based on the belief of the reality of the third dimension. It is strictly an earth/astral plane phenomena where we can see other life patterns as if they are in a different time zone, and we call this mental experience reincarnation. The whole idea of lineal lives creates a wrong impression of reality.

From the earth plane we can tune in to any other vibration, and it becomes reality because we see it as a now experience. We apply our remembered identity to the experience and call it a past life. We could easily be linking in to another facet of our own higher self.

We create our own reality wherever we are, and we have to remember that we are creating the past and future from the now. The same is true of cause and effect. The belief in the succession of elements of time give the effect of association of events, or time and space.

If we redirect our attention away from the present moment, we will have some kind of mental experience. We immediately apply a time structure to it, based on where we think it fits. We categorize all experience according to our recall of a similar experience. There is a similar time structure in the next level of awareness, the astral plane.

In the dream state, thoughts arise, have duration, and pass. This is precisely the same experience that we have of life here on earth. People have visions of things on the next level of existence, and the UFO experiences are examples of this kind of phenomenon.

A person experiencing a UFO has extended his sensitivity of consciousness and has allowed himself to break through into another dimension of time. The UFO is seen with the physical eye because the person has transferred his sense of reality to another level. It becomes so real to the observer that he has actually entered into that time and space. It is as if he is bi-located and able to experience two levels of awareness at the same time. The physical body does not enter into the future state, and those who think they have been touched have had a mental experience, not a physical one. Such experiences as stigmata and transfiguration are similar to the incidents experienced in UFO sightings and abductions. The physical body experienced in an operation by these astral beings is an imaginary one. It is similar to the body we use in the dream state. The experience may be true, but it is not a physical one.

The time frame we are living in is merely one of many. It is one chosen for this lifetime, and we bring our whole self awareness into this dimension so that life can be experienced to the fullest. It is only when we return to a higher level of consciousness that we become aware of the many directions our beingness has experienced, and all the resulting experiences come together to create our whole being in that higher dimension. In the dream state, we often share experiences with people who are either alive on earth at this time, or have died and left the earth. They are real to us in this next state, and whether they are living on earth now is inconsequential to the reality of the moment we are sharing with them.

Time is a mental experience made real by our beliefs in the reality of this life, and we create time to measure this life and give this experience some credibility.

CHAPTER TWELVE

LETTING GO

*A*S WE TRAVEL A SPIRITUAL PATH, we find many conflicting theories about life upon the earth and the afterlife. This is natural because every religion is the result of some person's interpretation of what is the truth about reality.

Like everything in life, we outgrow the ideas we have as we go along, and the things we thought were once so essential seem to lose their importance. This is especially true of spiritual philosophy. Each religion seems to have some elements of faith in a supreme being, and if we adhere to their particular teachings and stop seeking elsewhere, we can find some peace of mind when we attend their church.

Most religions would have us look outside of ourselves for some form of a God, which is represented by some figure, symbol, or book. The idea of God being an idea within us is seen by many people as a terrible blasphemy, and we soon find we are alone in our search for truth. We find that within most religions there are splinter groups that break away from the original teachings. Somehow all the different religions seem to lack permanence.

After a while, we get used to the idea that our trip is very personal, and we take ideas from each set of teachings that seem to make sense to us. We find that there are many gods to choose from, and we realize that any god is merely a representation of our own higher self. It is part of the great illusion of this dimension. As we are able to create our own reality, we can also create god in any form. History demonstrates this truth.

Many groups worship some tangible physical object and endow their god with different degrees of mystical power. We build massive temples, pyramids, and other icons to worship. We wear religious objects to remind us of our faith and read ancient testaments of religions from the past. All of this endeavor eventually brings us back to the reality that we are the final judge of what is spiritual for us.

I would like to pass on some teachings I have received from spirit guides who are willing to explain some of the things we will find when we start our own quest for truth of other states of beingness. These teachings come from a group of guides for whom I have great respect. I will quote these teachings exactly as they were given, because I think they are important:

> *We want you to realize that you have never left the spirit world, you have merely changed your orientation and are locked into the third dimension. It is just that you must have this third dimension for your physical being.*
>
> *This truth will help you understand that all dimensions are right here within this beingness at this time, in this world that you have here. It is merely that your mind is expanding as your perception becomes larger, which is easier for you in this physical being to understand, because you understand your physicalness which does not exist in the spirit world.*
>
> *I want you to know that we will be using analogies and comparisons, because you could not understand that in your physical terms you are as nothing, because the real you is not a physical being. There is no physical on our side. You, at this time, could not comprehend what your true beingness is,*

without your physical beingness with which to assess it. Here upon the earth plane you have your physical form and your belief in the different dimensions and the apparent solidity of things.

To understand this you need to experience what it is like in other states of consciousness where there is existence, but not in the physical sense. At the level from which I am speaking you are merely your own self, and your beingness is as light and love. So you can see that it is hard for us to explain what exists here in spirit if you are unable to experience it and use it as a comparison with the earth plane.

Those of you who have an out-of-body experience or a near-death-experience will understand because you will have left the physical world for a while and experienced our world for a short time.

Some of those in spirit from a higher level of consciousness have decided not to incarnate on to the earth plane. They can easily obtain the experience we have on the earth plane on other levels of awareness. However, there is a need for some of these higher beings to come here to be an example to us and to show us what is available in their world on the other side of the veil. They have achieved the same growth, the same love for others as the great spiritual teachers of the past.

We are inspired to be as they are, to become a part of them and bring their power into our own auric field. If we can achieve those same qualities, then we can become as spiritual a being as they are while we are on the earth plane.

To be a spiritual being in this world does not mean we have to be different. It merely means we will be able to bring more of the spiritual forces to the surface as we attempt to serve others. Within each person is the way to the great truth. There are no barriers except those we believe are there.

We enter this world as an individual spark of the divine essence and develop characteristics which create the personality that we think we are. This is the image of ourselves that we take as we leave this world and return to the next level of awareness. In this next level we can create images of ourselves as we wish. However, we maintain the earthly image for purposes of recognition by those we wish to meet.

We can turn this on or off at will, and it is interesting to experiment when we are out of our body. When we are aware that we are dreaming, we can mentally change our self or our surroundings. For example, if a person dies with a disfiguring disease or accident, they are quickly taught to recreate the image of themselves in their prime.

We can show the disfigured image of ourselves for purposes of recognition, then change so that our loved ones can see we are fine. The image we portray of ourselves in the next world is as transitory as this one. We go through many changes on our trip home. Eventually we are redefined from within until we become a being of love.

These conditions are not reserved for special beings. They are the goal of us all. We are striving to become as spiritual as the teachers are.

The guides look at our struggles on this plane with great affection. They shake their heads in disbelief sometimes, but they realize that we will eventually become as they are.

It is not an easy task to be a guide, and I have drawn up a list of duties a guide has agreed to perform for the person they have volunteered to coach.

ROLE OF A SPIRIT GUIDE

People usually begin a spiritual quest after some significant event such as a vision of a spiritual being, or the loss of a loved one. The spontaneous awareness of a person from spirit, even if it is a ghost, may come as a result of heightened sensitivity, or the feeling that this life is not spiritually satisfying.

Such an event will sometimes encourage the person to get in touch with a teacher on earth. This often results in the person also getting in touch with their teacher or guide from spirit.

This guide has to try to steer the person to the things that they need to achieve the self-fulfillment they are seeking in this dimension. If the student is able to converse with the guide, the guide will:

1. Enlighten the student to know what is really going on. If the student had a vision, the guide will explain how and why this occurred. After a consciousness expansion experience there is often a feeling of depression and disappointment.

   With people who have had a near-death-experience, this is particularly noticeable because they are usually not on a spiritual quest when they have their experience.

2. A guide will advise the seeker what attitude to assume in discussions of their psychic and spiritual experiences with other people who doubt him.

3. He will explain why there is an increase in all kinds of emotional experience. The rush of psychic power is often very disturbing. Entering a higher vibration may cause physical changes which we are not expecting.

4. Teach how to assimilate the powers coming from a higher source and teach how to channel the power for service to mankind and spiritual progression for the student.

5. Help to restructure the personality around the newfound higher self. To be aware and careful of spiritual pride.

6. To keep alive the vision of self-realization with its promise of serenity, joy, inner security, and radiant love.

This is not done in verbal exchange, except in special cases. It is done by guiding the student to situations in life which bring out what is required for growth. He or she may be guided to a book, a special guide, or be encouraged to meditate. Notice that there is always a choice of acceptance or refusal to follow these suggestions. The alternatives are always there. The decision is up to the student. The guide never interferes with the student's free will. No one can ever say that spirit made me do something. That is why we must ask for help before we can receive it.

A person who is doing something spiritual, such as healing, will have many helpers who will be on call. In some situations the healer will be a trance medium, and the guide will be able to speak directly to the patient.

In my work as a rescue worker, I have several helpers who bring those in need to me for counseling. My own guide rarely speaks directly to me, but he will strongly overshadow me.

He is able to convey what he wishes me to do in the work, whether it is leading a circle, speaking to a group in church, doing rescue work, or healing. He calls on many helpers, who I have seen and heard. I have complete confidence in the relationship we have established, without the need for words or visions.

I often send up a thought to him and thank him for his support and guidance. I wish we all would occasionally think of the ones who are always there to help and guide us.

CHAPTER THIRTEEN

REINCARNATION

WHEN WE START THE JOURNEY from what is called the Godhead, we enter into a series of vibration levels that we must pass through in order to reach the level of beingness we desire. At that time we are a speck of energy radiating with tremendous power from the source of "All That Is."

In this higher level, we do not assume a form that would be recognizable to anyone on the earth plane. It is only in the levels closer to the earth plane, where people on the earth are able to see us, that we assume an identifiable form.

The purpose of our incarnation determines the vibration level we adopt. This time we have chosen to pause for a brief period in the earth plane vibration.

Once established in this level of consciousness, the highest level that we could see is probably the first level of the spirit world. This is beyond the level known as the astral plane. Beyond the astral level we would need to make a consciousness shift to another level of awareness. There are some mystics on earth who have achieved this ability, but they tend to shun publicity.

There are beings at these upper stages who have such a high concentration of energy that we in physical form would not be able to be in their presence. The power that they have is so strong that even a minute portion of it would be destructive to us. If we were able to make the necessary adjustments in our vibrations, we would be able to share those same energy levels.

We can get glimpses of these higher levels while we are on earth, but it is rare for the average person. A deep meditation experience would be necessary for this to occur. Many people have a spontaneous mystical experience and disregard it, thinking it is a mental aberration, such as hallucination.

This is hard for us to comprehend, but the beingness at these higher levels is so different to what we have here. At the higher levels, these beings have no purpose that we would understand. Their purpose is purely creation and direction of the essence of the life force present in all things. They are in a totally different level of existence from what we are experiencing.

Our purpose in coming to this plane is service to mankind, and to seek enrichment and fulfillment to become a whole being. To achieve these goals and for us to remain in this dimension, we have developed an ego which acts as a divider between the levels of awareness.

As we move closer to this earth plane, we begin to understand more clearly how this whole process works. We have started out as a small speck of energy and we are given the opportunity to expand ourself. When we eventually return to spirit, we will have expanded through this growth process. Also, as we go back to rejoin the God force, we will have made ourself richer in a spiritual sense, and we will be adding the result of all our experiences to this main creative force.

This is really a very simplistic explanation of what is taking place, but we are limited as to what we can comprehend while we are on this earth level. Denial of these truths makes life much easier to live on the earth plane, and we can make materialism our goal without guilt.

We create our own personality through what we choose to accept when we enter this earth experience. As we develop our personality, we find it is easy to blame earth conditions such as our parents, our culture, or other physical conditions for anything we don't understand or approve of. At this stage we are not aware that we create our own reality and bring about the circumstances that create these conditions.

At the higher levels we would be living in a state of unconditional love. At some point we begin to prepare for our journey to this earth plane. From the moment we decide to separate, we begin to lessen our spiritual powers, for each level has its restrictions.

As we pass through each of these levels, there is a trace element of us that remains, as if we make a psychic imprint of our contact. This creates a link with each of the planes, and we can always use these links to remind us of our divine heritage.

It isn't possible for us to come to this earth plane as this small spark of energy. We come down from this higher level, and when we reach what would be about five levels above the earth plane, we then begin to divide ourself into many facets.

The higher self manifests through these various identities. Some of these facets will remain in the spirit world, others will experience the astral plane, and many will incarnate to the earth. Each of these facets gravitate to the level that is appropriate for them to receive the greatest amount of support for their quest to serve mankind.

Each facet is given independence, and each person does not have to take each one of the lives represented by these facets. These off-shoots from our main being experience the lifetime here that has been designated, and they adopt the appropriate time sequence for the period they have entered.

The earth and astral planes are almost interchangeable. We experience the astral when we sleep or have any extension of our sensitivity. This whole process is very simple, and it gives rise to the belief in lineal reincarnation.

There is no lineal succession of lives for any one facet, and as all is NOW, reincarnation has no validity beyond the physical/astral plane. Reincarnation is a useful subject for a discussion of the variety of experiences our total self is capable of having. However, the past and future are all being lived by various facets, and we have selected this particular vibration and time in which to experience life. We can experience other lives by extending our sensitivity, but we would be observing them, not living them.

There are levels of awareness where the oneness of all things can be fully understood, but at this earth level it is an intellectual concept only.

We usually look to the past when we look to other lives, and do not look to the future. As we live in a point of time, in a long continuum of time, the future has already been lived for some beings. Our higher self is already reaping the benefits of past, present, and future times, and it is in contact with all those periods. This is all happening just a few steps above where we are now.

When we come to this level, we pause, and we begin to spread ourself for various purposes. By doing this, we are given this opportunity to expand our own energy force, gather more experience, and bring back a greater amount of spiritual growth to our core being.

When we cross over from this earth plane level, we have to go through quite a few steps of consciousness raising before we can even comprehend what takes place on some of these levels. This whole process is truly magnificent, and there is a feeling that there is a grand design to this universe.

One mystical experience of the oneness of all things is all that is needed for complete understanding of the process.

As we come through these different planes of consciousness to begin our work here on earth, we will experience some changes within ourself. We may be aware of physical or psychic changes as we grow spiritually.

These planes are much closer to this level here on earth than we realize. They are only two or three steps above us here. After crossing over to the next plane, we may decide that we would like to be a guide and work through a medium here for one lifetime. Therefore, that facet of ourself will have experiences within the astral plane to prepare us for the task.

As a guide, we would be doing work which would be similar to the guidance we have been receiving from our own guide. We sometimes help with those who are just crossing over or those who have already been over and are in need of help from guides or rescue workers.

If we choose to return to the earth plane, we must accept the same level of living conditions as the plane we are contacting. We may have come to the earth plane with the intent of bringing on earth the love we know is in spirit, but we are conditioned by the environment as soon as we arrive.

We can also decide before incarnating that we do not wish to have experiences in human form. Then we can work on other levels such as the planes which are right below us. It is not required for us to always take on these physical lives for the expansion of our self.

This is basically and very simplistically what we are seeking by coming to this level. After we feel that we have been given the chance to experience all of the things we started out to do, then we start on our return journey to our whole self.

Very simply, that is the process of our incarnation here. We become fascinated by the attractions of the third dimension and often do not return to the higher self immediately after a life here. There are many reasons for this. They range from intense love, to intense anger and hatred.

Such intense feeling will cause a person to incarnate again. Usually those with an intense love and desire to find another person will wait in the astral plane for a time and then go on to spirit and find their loved one there.

Those who have intense anger and hatred will incarnate again and again until they have outgrown those feelings developed on earth. This is one of the reasons that violence persists. It is possible for someone to outgrow anger on the astral plane, but it has to be achieved before it is possible for them to go on into the spirit world.

Sometimes a loving person will incarnate to share a life with an angry person, to try to get them to change their attitude and perception and look to the light. Eventually the person will be able to return to the spirit world, free of attachments to the earth. For some people, it takes a long time in earth years, but no one is lost for ever.

The astral plane is the center of activity for all emotions and earthly desires. Any negative characteristics must be left behind on these lower planes before the person is able to enter the spirit world again.

All that is necessary for those lost on the astral plane is to redirect their perception to the light of the spirit world. All the petty differences will be resolved by the guides who work with them.

I usually advise people not to expect or anticipate another incarnation unless they really want to return here on earth.

Anticipation or curiosity is setting the stage for reincarnation. Some people return here for altruistic reasons. From the spirit world we are aware of the state of life here with its hatred and violence. We feel we can change things by bringing on earth our love of peace and brotherhood. Thus, we try again. How simple it would be if the veil created by us could be removed. Mankind would see his real self, and there would not be any further need for this plane to exist. Despite such wishes, this plane is exciting and can be beautiful. Love flourishes throughout the world, and we are slowly becoming a more spiritual people.

If each person could take care of his own area of life and bring love to the fore, things would be on the right track. The world is the creation of our predecessors, and we are striving to make it a spiritual haven. To date we are on a spiritual path, and I hope we are adding our blessings to the efforts of those who are striving to change things for the better.

The great technological advances in science and medicine are of no avail if we are going to continue to promote hatred of our fellow man and incite war.

CHAPTER FOURTEEN

RESCUING LOST SOULS

*T*HE ASTRAL WORLD has an extremely wide range of purposes. These range from the entry to the light of the Spirit world, to the area that I call the "Dark and Dirty" levels of the fearful. Souls can trap themselves for thousands of years of earth time if they believe they are to be punished for something they have done in their previous life.

A being can create a barrier behind which to hide, and spirit helpers are unable to get to them to set them free. In this case, it is sometimes easier for spirit to exert influence on the soul to bring them to an earth plane contact who is willing to counsel them through a trance medium. These people are called Rescue Workers, and they volunteer to work with the lost souls and encourage them to progress to the light.

The main thing the rescuer has to get across to the soul is that there is no punishment except that which is created by themselves. These souls, like everyone else, have to live with who they are until they outgrow their self-imposed conditions of guilt and fear. Some will demonstrate bravado and arrogance and claim they don't care, but their attitude is based on loneliness caused by fear of interaction with other people.

Because the next world is a continuation of this life experience, the last thoughts we have prior to transition are the ones we use to recreate the next world. As there is no death, a person can have many different reactions to what he perceives in the astral plane. Most people are not aware of the fact that they create their own reality by the thoughts they think.

There are many situations where a person dies and is not aware of the fact that he is no longer on the earth plane. For example: the people killed at the World Trade Center in New York had no idea they were going to die when they went to work that day. Anyone killed from a sudden explosion, a person who dies in his sleep, a person killed by an accident, or from sickness, is a candidate for help from people still on the earth plane.

Some folks believe they are still on the earth plane and will open up to a helper who is still alive and reject people in spirit. Some people think they are hallucinating, and in a way they are. The image-creating ability of the soul in the Astral World will manifest their thoughts, and these creations seem very real to them.

The environment we find ourselves in when we make our transition is determined by the spiritual growth we have achieved in the past, and we automatically gravitate to a level of awareness conducive to our particular vibration. Everyone goes to heaven, depending, of course, on what their idea of heaven is.

We stay at this level until we realize we have died, and we reassess our fundamental beliefs in survival of the human spirit and of who we are. Suicides have some problems adjusting to the fact that there is no death, no matter how hard they try to kill themselves.

Prisoners will still believe they are in prison, for that is their mind set when they died. They will reincarnate as soon as possible, full of hatred and wanting revenge unless they are counseled before they have the opportunity to return to earth.

When we die, we will probably explore this astral plane and the use of any new-found powers. The realization that we have the ability to go anywhere by a change of perception needs to be learned and understood. The creative ability of the mind, whereby we can manifest anything we wish, is cause for some experimentation on the part of newcomers. However, we will outgrow the novelty of these powers and feel more comfortable once we are free of the more recent earth-plane memories.

Newcomers to the fourth dimension may try to contact loved ones back on the earth plane to reassure them that they are still alive but in another world. It is sometimes disturbing for a soul in spirit to learn that people on earth cannot hear or see them, and they may try to get the attention of a loved one. Many widows have sensed the presence of a deceased husband.

When we die, most people are met by loved ones and are helped to adjust to this new life experience. However, some people are unaware that there is no death, and if they have done some things that they believe are bad, they may be ashamed and try to hide. Some people have regrets about what they have done and are carrying a lot of guilt. Some are vindictive and wish to punish the ones who have harmed them.

Finding they are still alive, some souls think they are still on the earth plane. It is difficult for the members of the family in spirit, or the guides, to work with them because they are still looking into the earth plane. Sometimes it is easier for the guides to influence them to come to a rescue worker for counseling.

The first thing to be understood by the newly deceased is that this new life is a continuation of the old one.

Next, we must learn that everything material from the earth has gone. The only things we take with us when we pass are our memory and our character. This means we can recall some significant events that have occurred during this earth life. The quality of our character determines our evaluation of these memories. We quickly learn that we have created the world we find ourselves in.

When we look back on this life, we can recall many instances of good, and not so good, things that we have done. Some of the things that we may not be proud of seem to stand out clearly, and most of the good things seem to fade into obscurity. Such is the nature of our self-concept. We have all done things we would not like to see printed in the newspapers.

Some people have done hurtful things to others, and when they find that there is no death, and they have to live with what they have done, they may try to hide. Eventually they may try to put right the wrongs they have done and will try to contact the victim to apologize. One man asked me how he could contact three women he had stalked, to tell them he was sorry. I told him he would have to wait until they came to spirit, and then the contact would be up to them. I felt he had bothered them enough. Many people expect to be judged and punished because that is the nature of the Christian religion. Some people believe we may go to some heaven or hell because we were supposedly born in sin. If we believe in heaven and hell, we are living it right now, for that is the belief system by which we judge ourself and view the world.

In the next world there are many people who try to help these souls. However, everyone has free will, and they can mentally create barriers that prevent others from getting close enough to help them. When these souls realize they are still alive, they believe they are still connected to the earth plane in some way. A rescue worker is still on the earth plane, and lost souls will usually relate to someone still on earth.

We all have a spirit guide who has been with each of us since we entered this world. He or she will stay with us until we are free of attachment to the earth plane. This means that when we release someone's attachment to this life, we also free a guide who is committed to helping.

The guides have always been trying to influence us to do what is best for us to reach our self-fulfillment, and this continues in the astral plane of awareness. A guide does not spend every moment looking over someone's shoulder. They keep in touch through telepathy, and are constantly available to help.

This next plane or level is an ideo-plastic world where our thoughts are immediately manifested as real. Consequently, a soul can hide for many earth years, literally looking into the past. This is the wrong direction, because they are hanging on to the memories and giving those memories renewed power.

On the earth plane we are protected by the fact that we can hide behind the personality that we express to the world. On the astral plane a person cannot hide. A rescue worker on the earth plane has to get the person to realize that there is no judgment and direct him to go to the light.

As a rescue worker I usually meet with the mediums individually. At this time I am working with two wonderful volunteers. We usually meet once a week, and there are usually about ten cases handled during each session. My role is to counsel the people who come through; so, obviously, I depend on the mediums. They are the real workers in this situation.

It is fascinating work for me, especially the type of character that I sometimes have to deal with. It is difficult to make some people understand there is no death. However, I know I am performing a service for both the guide and the person in need of help.

Of course I am not alone in this work. One of my guides in spirit, Brother Joseph, goes out into the planes of desolation and somehow influences these lost souls to come to a rescue worker for help. The medium's guide will then decide who will speak to the rescue worker. As I am completely unaware of the person who will come through, my first question is for their first name. Then I find out what their problem is.

In spirit there is a wonderful team of people who are always in evidence when I am working with any of the mediums. I have been told that there are many souls who help, but there are four helpers who speak to the souls getting help from me, they are:

Mark Osborne: He was a teenager who was high on drugs and rode his bicycle into the wire holding up a mast on a school yard. When he got to spirit, he asked the guides if he could help kids like himself who had overdosed on drugs. He came to me and told me he had no relatives in spirit and asked me to work with him whenever he brought these "druggies" to a session. He is often present when a drug victim comes through, and the victim is usually angry at being pestered by Mark to go to the light.

Sister Mary: She is a beautiful nun who radiates light and always appears when I am working with children. The children will often say she is an angel. When she comes to a child, she is always accompanied by children of the same age as the one I am working with. I asked her once why she is always the one who comes for the children, and she told me there are many, many souls who work with the children and she is only a representative of them.

Father Ralph: He was a Catholic Priest and he has volunteered to appear for all Catholics who die without receiving last rites. Many Catholics who die in circumstances such as an air crash or other accident will believe they have to go to purgatory. They will mentally create some kind of existence which they believe represents purgatory, and they want to wait for some ritual to release them. There is no such place as purgatory or hell, and I try to make people understand they create their own reality. If I am unsuccessful, I send them on to Father Ralph who appears when I send out a thought for him. He gives them what they think they need.

Dr. Bill: He was a doctor in a San Francisco AIDS hospital, and he came to me one day asking if I would work with him to help AIDS victims to get to spirit. Of course I said I would, and he said he would come whenever I have an AIDS victim who refuses to acknowledge the fact that he is dead. Many AIDS victims have been rejected by their family and society in general. When they die, they have a tendency to close off into a state of seclusion, and they may refuse to speak to me. Dr. Bill, or one of his nurses, will appear in their uniforms, and the person, believing he is still in hospital, will open up to them and will go on into spirit.

A rescue work session is not a seance. The room is brightly lit, and usually there is only myself and the medium present.

The medium will withdraw her consciousness as if going to sleep, or into a hypnotic state. People who have had a past life experience, or been hypnotized, will have experienced the same kind of thing. The person in spirit is able to project his or her concepts to the medium's aura, and the medium interprets them into language. No one can enter the medium's body.

Every person is totally inviolate. Every thought we have, especially fear, is the result of our belief system about reality. The idea of possession is for television and comic books. A person can become obsessed by an idea, but that is not possession. It is a psychological identity problem requiring professional help.

A student of yoga came to me insisting he was occasionally possessed by a grotesque evil spirit. I tried to explain he was creating the being, based on his guilt, and he gave the thing power whenever he thought of the past. He would not accept my idea, and I feel sure he is still carrying his guilt. This subject of how we create our own reality is covered elsewhere in this book.

This whole rescue work process is done by mental telepathy. The person coming through is from a parallel world and is limited to communication only. In the past, the mediums have had no memory of any of the contacts, but recently there has been a change and some of the mediums are now able to participate in the process. This is helpful, as the rescue worker can obtain more information quickly and speed up the process.

Let me close this chapter by reminding you that death is nothing to fear. The future is a continuation of this life without the pain and suffering. Wonderful help is available to all when we finish this life, and we will see our loved ones again.

Whatever service you are doing in this lifetime, and whatever you are able to find in your own heart of the living spirit and living truth, keep doing it. If you can find within yourself some joy, humor, and compassion, and you can look at all the suffering in the world and keep your heart open, you will know you are on the right track. Do what you can in terms of service to mankind and acknowledge the perfection of the grand design.

CHAPTER FIFTEEN

OVERVIEW FROM SPIRIT

RECENTLY I RAISED A QUESTION with one of the spirit guides concerning emotions in spirit. The reply I got was quite extensive and interesting. I thought I would include that information in the book.

A guide had previously stated that there were no emotions in spirit, for the simple reason that everything was produced by thought. I remember some years ago at a regular meditation meeting there was a lot of laughter in the group. A guide came through and said he thought he should take an incarnation so that he could develop a sense of humor and enjoy our atmosphere as we did. When asked by one of the sitters what he meant, he said there were no such emotions in spirit, they were not necessary.

I knew at that time that the mind created everything in the dream state and the astral plane, because I was having out-of-body-experiences and had learned how to change the atmosphere in the astral plane. However, many people I speak to in rescue work are bitter, angry, vengeful, and resentful. They may be full of hatred toward the person who may have killed them. Hence the question, what is an emotion if it is not the things I just mentioned?

Of course the guide had a very simple explanation.

Surrounding the earth plane is an area that spirit does not regard as a separate plane. This area is known as the emotion and desire plane in the Eastern philosophies, and spirit regards it as a part of the earth plane. This is where we begin to divest ourselves of all connections to the earth plane and prepare to enter the first level of the spirit world.

This astral area is also viewed by spirit as a temporary resting place for souls in transition after leaving this world. Many people coming to spirit after an incarnation here need an adjustment period because they have become totally infatuated with this world. They often think they are still on earth and have to learn of their transition to spirit.

Some folk take longer than others to get acclimated to the new conditions, and it is not unusual for people to dwell here for hundreds of earth-time years. They are completely unaware of the passage of earth time and sometimes are unaware that there is no death.

More spiritually knowledgeable people do not dwell here for long. If they have a belief in an afterlife, an acceptance of survival, and they are expecting to be met by relatives, loved ones, or guides, then they pass very quickly into the light of the spirit world.

This makes sense, because the area of consciousness for dreams, other out-of-body experiences, hypnotic trance, and clairvoyance are viewed by us using a slight variation of our earthly senses. Most of the other levels of spirit call for a consciousness shift to another level of awareness, which is a different mind-set than we have here on earth.

In this first area of the astral we meet loved ones who have been expecting us, and they quickly take us to the appropriate level of the spirit world. They appear in a form that we can recognize, although they can show themselves in any form they wish.

One of the promises I offer people who are being rescued is that they can lose old age and be whatever age they wish when they go to the light. Also they will lose any physical sickness or other disability. I remind them that the spirit is perfect, ageless, and indestructible because we are all immortal.

The people I help in rescue work hang on to the idea of their physical body and have to be taught that they create their own reality, including their own body.

This first non-physical state of awareness is composed of mind stuff, which is ideo-plastic. It is like a cloud of energy which manifests the thoughts of the observer. This is completely new to the recently deceased, and they need time to get used to it. Once they accept this, they are free to explore the new powers that go with this new life.

Most people do not hang on to this duplicate body for long, unless they are afraid, or completely unaware of the fact that they are dead.

I think we should continue to use the term "astral plane" for this area, as it follows directly after we leave this world. To most people on earth it seems to be a separate plane or level of experience. The term spirit, or spirit world, could be reserved for the various levels of the spirit world that follow the rest period in the astral plane.

One guide told me that before entering the area of the light that we see at the end of the tunnel, we must be ready to divest many of our associations with the earth plane. We are then ready to experience the first of the seven levels of the spirit world. He said he would discuss them one by one in the future.

He explained that when he comes to talk to us, he has to change his vibration to the level that we are used to, and that it is difficult sometimes.

He said that it is very draining, and he likened it to our being very tired after a long, arduous journey on foot when we feel we can't go another step. Many times in our meditation group we have noticed that when they draw close to us, we can feel either heat or coldness, depending on how well spirits are able to merge their vibration to that of the group. Many mediums report similar feelings.

Healers notice that, when they are healing and a guide comes in to assist them, their hands become hot and the patient will feel a heat stimulation from this energy. All these affects are strictly for the earth and astral planes. After a person leaves this first area, he will not have any of these earthly feelings at all.

It is hard for us to conceive of life without emotion. I asked the guide about love in the spirit world, and he said that love is not an emotion, it is a state of consciousness. We can also tune into this level and project love from within us because we are already in touch with that level.

The seven levels of existence, after we reach the spirit world, are like a ladder of progression to become our whole self. Each level is a change of perception, and we outgrow each one as we progress. We are in the process of becoming a whole being in order to merge back into the higher self from which we came.

There is far too much to be learned in this world for one expression of the self. Therefore, the whole self has projected many different forms, or many different people, to experience all that can be had in this life.

When we arrive at about the third level of spirit, we will meet those other beings that we were, and still are, and we will recognize them as soul-mates. We are all part of a oneness, and we will know those beings that we have been in both the past and the future of earth time.

There is a meditation exercise using peripheral vision where we are able to see a succession of faces overshadow us. Many of these faces belong to aspects of ourself, and some are guides who wish to identify themselves. I see faces of Arab, Chinese, Indian, and others, showing various identities that I feel are part of the group soul of which I am a member.

There is not much difficulty in choosing which identity to assume. We are all part of the same higher self, and are on our way to the same spirit destination. We outgrow the need for an identity before we move on to the higher levels, so names and personalities are not important.

Some soul-mates are alive on earth now. Some are in the past and some are in the future, now. It is easy to see that the whole self is a composite being of all the different beings we have been and are. Eventually, we become one with all that is and individual identity is no longer required. Again, it is very hard for us to conceive of this condition, as we are firmly convinced that we are unique in this universe.

When spirit people come to the earth plane to communicate with us, they do not stay long because of the energy drain that takes place. The whole universe, regardless of various planes of consciousness, is composed of energy. The rate of vibration varies with each different plane, and as the speed of the energy vibration changes, it breaks down into color, sound, and mass.

The energy can be used and forms can be created by spirit to show themselves to us. We call this phenomenon "thought-form creation." When we see an apparition or ghost, we are seeing the thought form of someone who is creating a form similar to the one they had on the earth. They usually are unaware that they are doing this. It is just that they need to have a form to convince them they are still alive, although they are dead to this world as far as we are concerned.

When spirit beings come here, they do not see anything physical as they do not have physical eyes. It is important that we understand this. Some people think they are being watched all the time by people from spirit; this is not true.

When spirit people come to this dimension, they can interact with the aura of energy surrounding us. They can know if we are sick, or injured, or if anything is wrong. They know if we are having a problem by the disturbance of the energy field. They do not know what the problem is, but they do know that something has upset us. Spirit can only know what we direct to them by thought or prayer.

Much information of our emotional self is contained in the aura. Spirit can tell the state of our emotions of the person on earth by the quality of the colors in the aura. I am sure that most people have had moments when there is a feeling of a light radiating around them. This is a common feeling in the first level of the spirit world. Revelation and explanation of everything in this spirit-world level of pure unconditional love makes us feel we are home at last.

CHAPTER SIXTEEN

PASSAGE TO THE NEXT LEVEL

W HEN WE FINISH WITH THIS LIFE, we do not go anywhere, we merely change the direction of our attention. On earth we usually look out through the physical senses and focus on this third dimension. At death, the vehicle we have used here is no longer appropriate, so we dispense with it by removing our attention to another level and by severing the connection.

It might help if we can visualize a state of consciousness shaped like a flat plane of concentric circles. We have been concentrating on one of the outer circles, which we call the earth plane, and we are now withdrawing to another level. This level we can call the astral plane. It is still part of the earth plane, and we still think we are as we were, prior to transition. We still have our memory of the past life, and we also have our sense of who we are, our character. However, that is all we have.

The first thing we are made to realize is that we are still alive and this new life is a continuation of the old one. The environment is different, and there is a tremendous feeling of relief as if a weight has been lifted from our shoulders. Somehow age and sickness are no longer part of our consciousness, and we feel a sense of freedom.

There are some strange feelings arising within us as we change our perception from the earth plane and become aware of the astral plane. Earthly concerns begin to drop away, or are seen as not very important. Our sense of who we are changes, and we become more open to new ideas and experiences. There is a sense of awe at all we are going through, and there is an expectation that something wonderful is about to happen.

As we look out into this new dimension, we find there is a world experience similar to the world we knew before, except things change before our eyes. We find the environment changes rapidly, as if it is responding to our thoughts. We find we are in a cloud of energy that assumes forms from the thoughts we are having, and we realize we create our own reality by the thoughts we think.

Eventually, we have a thought in the form of a question such as, "Where am I?" This is immediately answered by the arrival of a being we can recognize, a person we have known from the past. It is probably someone who is surrounded by light.

We find we can adjust to the light and we recognize the being. It is usually a loved one or friend who has come to meet us, or it is someone we vaguely remember but can't quite place. This would be a guide or teacher we have met in our sleep or dream state, and we sense a compatibility with them, as if we know each other very well.

By some form of telepathy, they encourage us to go with them. We instinctively feel we should accompany them, and we leave the area of the astral plane and go toward a brilliant light up ahead. For some people the light is extremely bright, and we must focus for a few moments to adjust our vision. As we do so, changes begin to occur. This is the start of our passage to the spirit world.

Concerns for the people we have left behind are still with us, but we somehow know that everything will be taken care of. As we proceed toward this light, we feel we should be making some decisions about the past, and we must let go of many attachments.

This is a crucial time for us, and we begin to review our past life and decide what we may still be concerned about. If we mentally ask for guidance, it will be there instantly. We will be shown options, and we may decide to try and change something we have left undone on the earth plane. This has the effect of halting our progression.

We learn that the astral plane is where we outgrow these attachments to the earth plane. The astral plane responds to the will of the observer, and as we think, so it is. If we decide that it is necessary for us to remain in the earth plane vicinity, then we can remain in the astral until we learn to let go.

For example: A wealthy man leaves money to several relatives and does not approve of the way they are spending his hard-earned money. He may be very angry and want to influence them not to squander their inheritance. He can remain in the astral for many earth-time years and not realize that he has no reason to worry about money. There is no such requirement in the astral or spirit planes. The only medium of exchange is love.

The whole journey from the earth plane to the spirit world is one of enlightenment. We can see our past life and see our good and not so good experiences. We see some examples of behavior where we have been unkind that need resolution. We are able to see where the plans we made before we were born have been necessary for our growth.

When we have cleared away the thoughts of the past, we are ready to go to the light and enter the spirit world. We soon learn that we are on the first of seven levels or degrees of spirituality. Somehow we know there is a great adventure waiting for us when we are ready to proceed.

There is a great feeling of love around us, and we are encouraged to rest until we feel ready to learn more of this new life. Our guide or mentor, who has been with us throughout this past life, and the transition to spirit, lets us know that he is always available to help us.

The guide will stay with us until we make the shift to the spirit world. We are never alone once we leave this world, only unaware of the presence of our guide. He cannot interfere with our free will. We are the ones who make the choices, both here and in spirit.

If we meditate for a time each day, we will establish a contact with our guide, and he will be closer to us to help if we need him. Apart from the contact with our guide, meditation will bring a wonderful sense of a spiritual atmosphere that is always surrounding us. This is the confirmation we have been seeking—the divinity which comes from within us.

So look to the light when you are ready to make your transition. There you will find the love and happiness you gave up to come to this planet for the experiences you have chosen.

There is no such thing as failure on the spiritual path we are treading. All experience is part of the grand design of the universe.

CHAPTER SEVENTEEN

A JOURNEY OF ASCENSION

THE FIRST THING WE HAVE TO UNDERSTAND on a journey to the higher realms of consciousness is that we have to give up our sense of individuality. There are a number of people who have accomplished this in the past, and we regard them as masters or advanced beings. These are individuals who unknowingly have become selfless and have devoted themselves to service to their fellow man.

The selfless individual is the type of person who will perform some thankless task because it needs to be done, not for reward. They generally are not on some spiritual path, and they go about their lives without realizing the impact they have on the world around them. They have attained a very high degree of spirituality, but would probably deny any religious inclinations.

This is a level of beingness which is available to all of us, but mostly we do not wish to surrender to the prompting of the inner self. We are mostly unaware of the spiritual prompting and feel frustrated at the violence and greed around us.

On any journey to a higher realm we have to outgrow our desire to be on the plane where we are at present; that is what progress is. There is an inner urge to move on, especially in men, and we must make room for the new experience. Most of us have a place at home where we have things stored that we are not using, but we don't wish to discard them. Spiritual progression is the same. We must be prepared to let go of encumbrances.

Unfortunately, it is usually those little pleasures that we hang on to that make life bearable.

The ego is very strong, and we tend to resist letting it go. But ultimately, we have to surrender the self and become a part of the whole being, where there will be no need for individuality.

As we progress, all the planes that seem so important now will be lost. As we lose them, so our perception will change, and we will enjoy new venues and will be in the company of similar individuals who are also on the path.

The personality we exhibit at this time is just one of many facets of our own higher self that has divided into many personalities. This is to allow the whole being to more fully experience all possible variations of the creative life force, which is expressing itself through all that is.

Each of these variations of the self is individual, and they, or we, will eventually reach the point where we will begin to merge back into the oneness. We can experience the state of beingness when we are in the oneness through deep meditation.

We can know the sensation of total surrender in retrospect, but we cannot know the experience objectively while we are having it. Intellectually, we can accept the premise that all is one, but it takes an experience of the level of consciousness in the pure golden light to understand the meaning of the truth of the oneness of all things.

When we are entering the first level of individuality from all that is, we automatically divide a projection of the higher self into many facets. This shift into multiplicity allows the higher self to be aware of all levels of this third dimension.

Regardless of the personality being expressed through these different facets, there is the same composition of character traits. The emotions of the individual are the one variable that distinguishes the person and brings the different experiences back to the whole being.

The basic character trait that is fundamental to all people is love, and it will eventually become dominant. This love will urge the surrender of the self to the need for ascension back to the whole being in the higher realms. It is like a small voice of conscience reminding us of our heritage.

Most advanced beings are not concerned with their physical form. Their personality of love and service to others makes it easy for them to disregard the needs of the body. The fact that they took human form for this incarnation to fulfill some particular mission means they need an ego and physical form, but this is not their prime concern. Their primary concern is their mission.

As we outgrow our need for the ego, we see that some of our fellow travelers at the new levels of awareness are fewer in number compared to the mass of mankind on earth. It is not that they are special, it is merely that they are more aware of the spiritual potential within themselves. To us on the earth plane, the masters seem to be very advanced. Fortunately, they come to the earth plane as a model of the possibilities that we all have. We have within us the same love, the same unselfish giving to all others, that they exhibit. It is only when we are in their presence that we are aware of the feelings that arise within us and bring tears of joy to our eyes.

They repeatedly tell us that we are as they are. This is hard for us to believe, and we tend to deify them because of the love they have for all things and beings.

We can and do touch this level of love occasionally as we are enthralled in a magnificent cathedral, hear some inspiring words or music, or know the joy of too much tenderness. These are the moments when we can let go of the confines of the ego and enjoy a touch of the infinite. These are the moments when we have incorporated part of them into our aura and have lost our ego.

After one experience of the oneness, we know the nature of the universe, and all things fall into place. We know that all is right with the world and that we are all progressing to self- realization. It feels as if we are standing at the foot of a rising golden pathway, and we know that the higher self is at the end of this path. In future meditations we can use this symbol of the rising pathway to raise us to other levels.

We are also aware that we can never lose the knowledge we have gained from the experience and the wonderful feeling of peace that descends upon us. Regardless of what other people say or do to dissuade us from our path, we know we have seen the infinite.

This realization is what we have been seeking. There is a feeling that the race is over, and we know that eternity is now. We have always had access to it. We were focussed outwardly and unaware of the love and beauty that is within us.

From the newly acquired viewpoint, we can see how we may have come into this dimension to try and bring on earth the truths that are so prevalent in the higher realms. Unfortunately, we also see how we submitted to the current situation on the earth plane. So many people come into this earth plane with spiritual intentions and are caught up in the status quo.

To speak out against the basic trend of the planet that seems bent on self-destruction marks the mystic as a disturbing rebel. It is true that those who know the truth say nothing, and those that know nothing have much to say.

The exciting experiences of self-evaluation and growth have made the journey worthwhile. The reward has been the wonderment of self-realization and those moments of unity with the divine within the self.

These words are meaningless compared to the joy of the experiences mentioned above. Personal experience is the best way to learn the truth of our divine heritage, and meditation is one way to gain that experience.

CHAPTER EIGHTEEN

DEATH, WHERE IS THY STING?

*D*EATH IS REGARDED AS A TRAGEDY to most people because they are not aware that life is eternal. We naturally miss those who depart this world and go on to spirit. It is of course the physical presence we miss, because our loved ones are not able to share this life with us. It would be a tremendous help to most people if survival beyond the grave became part of our basic belief system.

Centuries of superstition and misinformation have caused mankind to dread the natural process of death. If we were raised with the truth that this body is a temporary housing for the eternal spirit, many fears would disappear. Our attitudes would be more friendly and our behavior more kindly. The thought that there are consequences resulting from our behavior would make us think before committing negative activities.

The design of this level of consciousness at this time calls for an atmosphere where negative activities can be played out. They have to be outgrown at this level before we can move on. If a person leaves the earth plane with anger, fear, or hatred, he will stay on the astral plane and reincarnate carrying the same conditions that he had while here.

Once free of this body and earthly attachments, our life continues. Consciousness in the next plane is enhanced and we have more power. In the dream state we can use these new powers, because we will have limited access to the spirit world.

The life force in the spirit world is never diminished. This is proven when we open ourselves to the higher levels of consciousness. On the earth plane we have very little idea of the power of the mind. For example, the power of faith used in prayer for spiritual healing and consciousness raising is not sufficient to convince the non-believer that there is a force greater than this earth.

When we are free of the restrictions of the limited faculties we have on earth, most people have regrets about the life they have led. Many people would have done some things differently had they known about survival. The so-called sins of omission and commission weigh heavily for a while, until the passing souls realize that those things belong to the earth plane, and they are now free of that environment.

Coming to spirit is a great revelation, and many things have to be clarified. Some of the main attachments on the earth plane are related to the many activities surrounding nourishment for the physical body. In spirit it is no longer necessary. We don't have to feed and clothe a physical body any more.

We will be able to change our surroundings by a change of thought whenever we wish, and we will be able to tune into any time period.

All that ever was, is, and always shall be, is available for inspection. We are not limited by time, space, and matter, as we are here on the earth plane.

It is helpful if we keep in mind that our departed loved ones are not far away. They are able to hear us if we feel like praying to them. Even a thought addressed to them will be received, and it need not be a prayer.

We may sense a touch and feel our loved one is nearby, for there is love in a touch or caress. Often a person in spirit will try to reassure a loved one left behind that he or she is fine. This transmission of love is quite possible. Love is the one power that transcends all barriers and is the greatest force we know.

We should not be concerned that our loved one is not whole again. All people in the spirit world are taught to be free of disability or disease as soon as they arrive. Shedding the physical body is like the snake that sheds its skin and gains a new one. The new one is free of pain and sickness, and there is a wonderful sense of freedom and renewal.

We should not be concerned that the departed one will not remember this life and all the details of our relationship—since the only things we take with us are our character and our memory. The loved one in spirit will also have a clarity of recall and access to information that we do not have.

We should not be concerned if we have a secret or two from our loved one. As soon as we depart this state of awareness, we begin to lose the negative aspects of this life, and we have a different level of understanding about all things. Since we move into states of awareness where only love is present, many differences are resolved, and we begin to understand why things happened as they did.

We soon become very involved in this new atmosphere of self-discovery, and memories of the pain or suffering that preceded our transition to spirit are soon forgotten. We will be fascinated by the ease with which we made the transition from earth to spirit and will wonder what all the fuss was about death.

We hear people say their loved one has gone to spirit. We are spirit right now in physical form, so where can we go? We merely withdraw our perception to another vibration rate. We often speak of people going to the "other side." The other side of what?

Many people speak of the veil, which I must confess appears impenetrable, but there is no such thing unless we believe there is. It is a self-created barrier to keep our attention here on the physical plane. The fact that we can penetrate this veil, when we sleep or go into an altered state of consciousness, proves it is easily crossed.

Some say their loved ones have died to the physical form and been born to the spirit form. We lose the physical form and become aware of the astral body that we have always had. But we on earth have not been aware of the spirit form.

We do not arrive in spirit in a chariot drawn by white horses, and sit on the right hand of you know who, and play music all day long on a celestial harp. However, if that is what people believe or want, that is what they will get. We create our own concept of reality, and the image-creating ability of the mind has free reign when we are released from this body.

Some believe that, when we die, everything ceases to function, as if someone has cut off the life force of humanity and the self no longer exists. If that is what they think, then they will be in darkness until they see the light, usually with the help of a rescue worker.

Eventually everyone catches on, but some need more help than others, and that is where the trance mediums and rescue workers come in.

Each person receives exactly what they expect when they go to spirit, simply because we create our own reality.

When people ask if their loved ones are all right, I usually tell them they are fine. Of course they are. They are doing whatever they are required to do, going where they need to go, walking their spiritual path, just as we are walking ours. The only difference being that we are in physical form and they are in spiritual form. They are advancing, and will be of help when the questioner arrives.

It is not so exciting as some of the strange tales told of the after-life. After this life there is a continuation. Some people believe that they will know everything when they arrive in spirit; not so. Knowledge still has to be acquired, and all knowledge is available for study and learning. Often there is a celebration by those who have preceded us as they welcome us to our new adventure.

If we can keep in mind that there is a love of God within us and our quest is to search this out for ourselves, then the way will be easier for both the departed and the survivors left behind. We are privileged to have access to the wisdom of the ages from the masters and teachers who come to help us. So take heed of them, for they are telling us the truth. Just be sure they are the real thing and that their ideas of truth do stand the test of reason, because some departed souls have not progressed spiritually as much as some people on the earth plane. As one master once said, "Apply all things to reason, even the things I tell you."

When we arrive in the astral plane, we are not handed a lot of secret knowledge on a plate. We all have to learn, and it takes time to discard our earthly belief systems. We still maintain our sense of humor, and sometimes a friend will play a joke on us. Since we are able to assume any form or identity in the astral plane, a person may claim to be someone they are not. Life in the astral plane is a continuation of this earth life. It is not a somber, miserable existence as some religious people would have us believe.

Occasionally a person will come through a medium claiming to be another person. Usually they are just testing to see if it is possible to communicate through a medium. I once asked one of the guides why they allowed this to happen. He said it is better to let them through briefly, because if they are stopped, they can become a nuisance.

When I am working with deceased people, I am always aware that some spirits are a little mischievous. As they are still close to the earth plane, they may be able to manipulate some physical energy and move objects around. This behavior is usually harmless, but it does frighten a lot of people. The energy they use can be produced by the exuberance of young people in the household. It is similar to the energy produced by the mental concentration of a group of sitters at a seance.

Some psychic phenomena may be the result of a person trapped in the astral plane who is unaware that he is dead. I recently had a situation where a man believed he was at a wedding reception. He had a massive heart attack and died. He thought the year was 1958 and was surprised that people at the reception would not speak to him. When he tuned into the light, he saw his parent, his wife, and all his children who had grown up and made their transition to spirit.

When I first began my investigations into psychic phenomena, I found it difficult to attend a movie theater. The atmosphere in a theater is perfect for a seance. There was a closely seated group of people, sitting in the dark, all intently concentrating on the screen. Around me would come voices from spirit. People looked around to see if I was speaking. Once it was so loud that I left the theater. In those days (the 1950s), my enthusiasm was very high and I was devoted to the study of mystical practices.

Spontaneous psychic phenomena of the kind I had experienced can sometimes occur when the conditions are right. Many people have had a psychic expeirence in a crowded church. The congregation are all concentration on spiritual matters, and there is often a powerful emotional state in the church. Death is nothing to fear, and there would be less suffering if this truth were widely known. The fear of death, and of the afterlife, has been fostered by superstition in the Western world.

Most of us will probably go through some form of distress prior to passing, but that is becoming easier with the advances of medical knowledge. Now there is no reason for a person to suffer intolerable pain.

I find that people have an easier time of crossing to spirit if they have accepted the truth of life after death. The knowledge that they will meet friends and loved ones is very reassuring. This also means that they will meet again with the loved ones they are leaving behind, and that is comforting for them.

I often advise the partners of dying people to give their loved one permission to go on. Know you will meet again. It is not serving any purpose for the patient to keep suffering.

Love does not die with the physical body, it is enhanced. The soul in spirit is free of the earth conditions, and their love is stronger because it is more concentrated on the person back on the earth plane.

How they would love to be able to tell their loved ones that they are safe and happy and waiting for the reunion.

CHAPTER NINETEEN

SPIRITUAL TRUTHS

WRITING A BOOK OF THIS NATURE raises many questions in the writer as well as the reader. When a question arose, I was fortunate to be able to refer to the spirit world for some interesting answers. When I was drawn to study the phenomenon of death, I came to this subject with an open mind, but with a lot of disbelief in the next world. Now there is no doubt in my mind of the truths included here, and I offer some questions and answers in anticipation that they may be of use to the reader.

1. First and foremost is the truth that there is no death.
   There is irrefutable evidence that we survive this life; in fact, it is impossible for us to die. We cannot even conceive of ourselves as being dead because we are always an observer and aware of being alive. When we die, we merely move to another level of consciousness and recreate an environment based on the last thought we had before we made our transition to the next life.

2. We create our own reality wherever we are.
   Each person sees the world in his own way. Each of us is an individual at this level, and we base that individuality

on our interpretation of the environment we are in. From the moment of our birth, we learn to accept that what we are told is reality.

Each person who has been born into this world, both past and present, is a contributor to the world as we know it. We all leave our imprint on the memory bank of the planet, and we are living with the result of all that has gone before into this universe.

3. We are attached to this dimension.

We are where our self-awareness is directed. In order to remain in this world, we accept the reality of this life, and we build up a belief system of what we consider reality to be. If we have a shift in our awareness, such as sleep or trance, the world ceases to exist for us. We assume that it will be there when we return, and it always is, until we finally make a separation from this life. This life is stable in this dimension for us because of our attachment here.

A study of the levels of consciousness surrounding the earth plane will reveal the fact that there are many different planes. There is life in various forms, from the supposedly solid form of the earth plane, to the fields of pure energy.

Immediately surrounding the earth plane is the astral extension of the earth, and this is a rest area to help in our transition to the spirit world. It is at this level that people realize they are dead.

After the initial period of readjustment into a non-physical world, we move into the first spirit plane and find there are seven levels of spirituality ahead of us. In this first plane we lose all of our attachments to the earth plane and become a spirit being.

On the second level, we begin to function without the image of a physical body, except for purposes of recognition by loved ones coming over to spirit.

In the third level, we meet the soul-mates who have been part of this projection of the higher self. We no longer identify with the earth plane consciousness.

At this point we begin to merge back into the oneness of all things, and we lose our sense of individuality. We are coming closer to our core being, and are being absorbed into the great essence of this creation.

4. We live in an energy field.

All matter is composed of atoms. Regardless of the outer appearance of things, all is energy manifesting in some form. Everything originates as a thought in the mind of someone or something, and the thought is made real using the substance that has been previously created.

Scientists can reduce all matter to its atomic energy state and can observe energy through powerful magnifying equipment. This scientific data supports the energy theory.

Mystics can also reach a level of consciousness where this energy field is visible to them by a shift in their awareness. Some Eastern religions refer to this substance as Mind.

5. We are all part of one substance.

Metaphysicians have found that there is a state of beingness where we are all part of a oneness. This is similar to the scientific energy theory. There is a state of awareness where we are no longer restricted to a physical form. Our individuality is a vibration of energy seen as light, which is a variation of love. Mystics say that love is the creative essence which we know as consciousness. We are always a being of some substance, and in the higher states we are formless as we have no need for a physical form. At the higher levels, all communication is by thought transference or observation of the aura surrounding a being. Consequently, no one can hide the nature of their being or attitudes from the helpers in spirit.

6. Meditation connects us with the Spirit World.

We should meditate daily, if only for a few minutes. By withdrawing our attention from the physical universe, including the physical body, it is possible to make a shift of consciousness to another dimension. Surrounding the earth plane is an energy level known as the astral plane, which is a part of the earth plane consciousness. This is the area we find ourselves in when out of our body in dreams and other conditions of unconsciousness. Exploration of this astral level brings confirmation of our ability to have life apart from the physical body.

Meditation also allows us to experience life in states of awareness free of the physical restraints. It provides personal evidence of life outside of this world. We experience this each time we achieve a consciousness shift to another dimension. Most religions suggest to their followers that they can contact some higher force by prayer or meditation, and they endow this higher state with infinite, divine powers.

7. We come here with a mission in life.

We come into this life with an intention to fulfill some mission we had in mind in the spirit world. We all set out to bring on earth the love we have known in the higher states from which we came. Unfortunately, we are immediately conditioned by the existing cultural life where we have incarnated.

8. We are our own judge and jury of our behavior.

There is no judge awaiting us when we die. We have to live with who we are, and that is punishment enough.

There is nothing but love beyond the astral plane, and it is the basis of all that is. Each being has free will to use the energies of this or any dimension to achieve their desires. Humanity sets standards of conduct called laws and claims that they are God-inspired. Religious writers set the rules for us, based on their ideas of right and wrong.

9. Eventually we come to love ourselves and all life.

First we must learn to love ourselves. We are radiating and creating the atmosphere around us, and we must accept who and what we think we are. We must be still, and know that the life force within us is the creative essence that is our link with the infinite. We each gravitate to the level of spirit to which we are attuned.

In the next state of beingness our thoughts are immediately manifested. We cannot hide any secrets because they are part of what we project as ourselves.

We come from a state of love in the spirit world, and we decide to bring this love to earth to try to raise the ideals and consciousness of all people on this planet.

10. We must all outgrow the earth-plane consciousness.

Visualize the mind state of a killer who is shot and dies from a police bullet. He arrives in the astral plane full of hatred, and his major thought is revenge on the person who killed him. He cannot wait to get back here to avenge his misguided idea that he is a victim and undeserving of what happened to him. To raise his consciousness to the light never occurs to him.

There are many like this, and they have this powerful force of hatred to keep bringing them back here. These same people come again and again to the earth plane. The only way to break this cycle is to change them in this world, and they will learn that they create their own problems. There is no war without warriors, no violence without hatred.

11. Personal responsibility.

We are responsible for our beingness. By the attitudes we have acquired, we develop a personality through living in this world. If we do not conform to other people's ideas of acceptable behavior, we are judged to be sinners. In the eyes of the world we should be punished, and there are many thousands of people who are incarcerated for various reasons. On earth there are many people who judge others and are willing to mete out punishment on those they believe deserve it. Whether we should punish others is an earth/astral plane question.

In the spirit world there is nothing but love. Each person is responsible for his own destiny, and in time this is realized. He will realize that he has to live with who he is, and that he has created his own problems.

12. Love is all in the Spirit World.

We find there is nothing but love awaiting us when we die and go to the light. We find there is nothing but acceptance of what we have done, because we have the experiences of the earth plane for our progression. We grow spiritually by outgrowing the need for the experiences we are having.

I have had many people in my rescue work sessions who have been waiting to be punished by God. They have difficulty accepting the fact that there is no one who wishes to harm them. Spirit is love. Hurt, pain, and suffering are for the earth plane.

Who is there to punish us? If you think you would like to punish the wrongdoer, then you have a problem. You would be playing God and would not have the full knowledge of reason behind the actions of others.

The idea of pain and punishment is so ingrained in the human psyche that people come to spirit expecting to be punished and will surround themselves with all kinds of protection so they can hide. These protections are possible because of the image-creating power of the mind.

13. We all outgrow the earthly experience.

No soul is lost forever. Regardless of the number of incarnations that we make, we eventually outgrow the need for the earth-plane experience. In our final earth-plane experience we would probably be born into a life of service, probably have no strong attachments, no surviving loved ones to be too concerned about, and we would probably die quite young. There would be nothing to keep us here, and we would be seeking a spiritual life even while we are here. We would probably avoid any religion that has a lot of pomp and ceremony in their services.

Many souls may have difficulty letting go of the earth-plane attractions, and they will stay on the merry-go-round of the wheel of rebirth until they understand that this life is not all there is. We have to go through whatever is necessary for our release from this earth plane. Unfortunately, negative-thinking people can be reborn again and again, and some have to live many times before they change.

14. There is a grand design to life.

These guidelines are not cast in stone, for we each have our own destiny planned. We always have freedom of choice, so we can change whenever we wish.

Through time there have been many changes in the thinking of man. Philosophies supersede each other, and our idea of reality has to keep pace with the new discoveries. Each person's thoughts contribute to the world-mind's idea of what is real. It is like a giant puzzle, and we all have a piece of the grand design of life.

This grand design seems to have a purpose, and all the changes come about in various ways. Some come through upheaval and violence, others by peaceful growth and development.

A universe so complex as the third dimension cannot be destroyed by the actions of a few people. The world will survive because reasonable people will contain the behavior of the destructive people.

We will all survive because there is no death. There will be many changes before we finally find the way to the light and the truth that is within us.

DARKNESS INTO LIGHT
Rescuing Souls on the Other Side
John L. Brooker
ISBN: 1-57733-094-3, 172 pp., 5.5 x 8.5, paper, $14.95
Rescue work with discarnate individuals is performed by trance mediums under the direction of guides from spirit and rescue workers on earth. Lost souls, unaware that they have died, are brought to a counselor who can help them understand their position and get them to move to where their loved ones are waiting for them.

SOMEONE ELSE'S YESTERDAY
The Confederate General and Connecticut Yankee:A Past Life Revealed
Jeffrey J. Keene

ISBN: 1-57733-134-6, 256 pp., 6 x 9, paper, $17.95
Someone Else's Yesterday is an amazing journey through the eyes of two people: one a Georgian, the other a Connecticut Yankee. Similarities between the two go far beyond coincidence. Jeffrey J. Keene is a present-day Assistant Fire Chief in Westport, CT. John B. Gordon, Confederate General, died January 9, 1904. Jeff Keene shares his insights into the workings of reincarnation along with his personal encounter with the nightmare of 9/1.

WHEN SPIRITS COME CALLING
The Open-Minded Skeptic's Guide to After-Death Contacts
Sylvia Hart Wright
Paperback, ISBN: 1-57733-095-1, 256 pp., 6x9, $15.95
Hardcover, ISBN: 1-57733-125-7, 256 pp., 6x9, $24.95
Never-before-published stories of apparent afterlife communication, told in the perceivers' own words. Comparing today's Western beliefs with those of other traditions, ancient and modern, Professor Wright opens the door to reasoned discussion about this often hush-hush subject.

OTHER BOOKS FROM BLUE DOLPHIN PUBLISHING

BEYOND DEATH
Confronting the Ultimate Mystery
Christopher Scott
ISBN: 1-57733-077-3, 244 pp., 6x9, paper, $16.95
From scientific, mathematical, and spiritual points of view, this books provides support for the continuance of life beyond death and for the Divine Mind that designed the delicate balance of elements from which life is formed.

YOU WILL LIVE AGAIN
Dramatic Case Histories of Reincarnation
Brad Steiger
ISBN: 0-931892-29-5, 248 pp, 5.5 x 8.5, paper, $12.95
Exciting case histories show how past lives are influencing the present—sometimes for the better, sometimes for the worse—but always for growth.

ENTITIES AMONG US
Unseen Forces That Affect Our Daily Lives
Catherine Bowman
ISBN: 1-57733-083-8, 168 pp., 5.5 x 8.5, paper, $14.95
Become aware of the subtle, intruding, detrimental energies generated by situations, people, places, and the astral plane. Step-by-step instructions are given to expel human parasites, astral debris, ghosts, and poltergeists.

O SANE AND SACRED DEATH
First Person Accounts of Death as received in hypnotic regressions
Louise Ireland-Frey, M.D.
ISBN: 1-57733-090-0, 272 pp., 5.5 x 8.5, paper, $15.95
Personal accounts of Near-Death Experiences and communications from "the other side" help people find the inherent beauty of death.

Orders: 1-800-643 0765 • www.bluedolphinpublishing.com

OTHER BOOKS FROM BLUE DOLPHIN PUBLISHING

YOUR MIND KNOWS MORE THAN YOU DO
The Subconscious Secrets of Success
Sidney Friedman
ISBN: 1-57733-052-8, 184 pp., 5.75 x 8.75, hardcover, $22.00

You will learn to tap into the subconscious, making its vast knowledge more readily available. More important, you will learn to feed it your wishes so it can help make them come to fruition. You will learn *The Subconscious Secrets of Success.*

THE SYSTEM FOR SOUL MEMORY
Using the Energy System of Your Body to Change Your Life
Susan Kerr
ISBN: 1-57733-089-7, 256 pp., 5.5 x 8.5, paper, $14.95

Soul Memory is the road map our higher selves use to present life challenges to us. If emotional energy is not cleared when it is first experienced, it is stored in a chakra. Energy that sits for a long time compacts until it becomes physical matter and is experienced as a physical injury or illness. *The System for Soul Memory* show how to keep your energy flowing freely, so your health will be excellent and you will be able to manifest your heart's desires.

THE ART OF LETTING GO
A Pathway to Inner Freedom
Vidya Frazier, L.C.S.W.
ISBN: 1-57733-112-5, 260 pp., 6 x 9, paper, $16.95

Vidya Frazier helps us discover a pathway to spiritual freedom that is simple and practical, yet powerfully profound. With gentle encouragement and compassion, she guides us in letting go of our mistaken identity with our ego and points to our true Self that is already free, here and now, living in peace and harmony with all that is.

Orders: 1-800-643-0765 • www.bluedolphinpublishing.com

9028101R0

Made in the USA
Lexington, KY
22 March 2011